Alien Encounters in the Western United States

Schiffer Publishing Ltd

4880 Lower Valley Road • Atglen, PA 19310

Tracie Austin

Illustrations by Kesara

In Memory of Budd Hopkins,
A Pioneer and Truth Seeker
Who Led the Way

Schiffer Books are available at special discounts for bulk purchases for sales promotions or premiums. Special editions, including personalized covers, corporate imprints, and excerpts can be created in large quantities for special needs. For more information contact the publisher:

Published by Schiffer Publishing, Ltd.
4880 Lower Valley Road
Atglen, PA 19310
Phone: (610) 593-1777; Fax: (610) 593-2002
E-mail: Info@schifferbooks.com

For the largest selection of fine reference books on this and related subjects,
please visit our website at
www.schifferbooks.com
We are always looking for people to write books on new and related subjects.
If you have an idea for a book, please contact us at
proposals@schifferbooks.com

This book may be purchased from the publisher.
Please try your bookstore first.
You may write for a free catalog.

In Europe, Schiffer books are distributed by
Bushwood Books
6 Marksbury Ave.
Kew Gardens
Surrey TW9 4JF England
Phone: 44 (0) 20 8392 8585; Fax: 44 (0) 20 8392 9876
E-mail: info@bushwoodbooks.co.uk
Website: www.bushwoodbooks.co.uk

Photographs provided by Steve Colbern and Dr. Roger Leir of A & S Research

Designed by Mark David Bowyer
Type set in Mona Lisa Solid / NewBaskerville BT

ISBN: 978-0-7643-4145-8
Printed in the United States of America

Contents

Acknowledgments

There are a number of people who I would like to give special thanks to. Without them this book would not have been possible.

Firstly, a grateful thank you to Dinah Roseberry and Schiffer Publishing, Ltd. for allowing me the opportunity to write this book, and to my editor, Dinah, and my designer, Mark Bowyer for all their hard work.

To my very dear friend, Dr. Roger Leir, for his first-hand accounts of the removal of alleged alien implants. Dr. Leir, you are the best, and a true pioneer of this incredible phenomena whose efforts are so valuable for uncovering the truth. You are so very much needed in this controversial and yet very real subject.

A warmhearted thank-you to Barbara Lamb, Certified Hypnotherapist and Regression Therapist, for her Foreword to *Alien Encounters in the Western United States*. Barbara, thank you for the truth that you bring to the abduction/encounter reality.

I would also like to give a very special thank you to my friend and extremely talented artist, Christine (Kesara) Dennett, for her commitment to this project, and her amazing ability to illustrate the alien beings as witnessed by numerous experiencers around the world.

Thank-you to Miesha Johnson of the Las Vegas Abduction/Experiencer Support Group, who graciously allowed me the opportunity of personally interviewing some of her members.

Note to the Reader

The following accounts of alien encounters are all true. *Alien Encounters in the Western United States* takes you on a journey of first-hand alien/UFO cases, with some of those mentioned being actual patients of Dr. Roger Leir, who documented their personal encounters and performed surgery to remove their alleged alien implants. But while the events are true, some of the names of the people involved have been changed to protect their identity, as the cases presented here reveal how the lives of these ordinary people were very much affected through interaction with the alien presence. I ask that you keep an open heart and an open mind as you read the following chapters of extraordinary, and very real cases of alien encounters!

"I look forward to the day when the secrecy surrounding Extraterrestrial contact ends so that our race can move forward to the next phase of its history – non cosmic in scale."

~Dr. Michael Wolf Kruvante

Ph.D, M.D., D.S.C., M.S., B.S.
Scientist, and Author of
The Catchers of Heaven

Foreword

From A Regression Therapist's Point of View

By Barbara Lamb M.S., MFT, CHT

It is a service to humanity that Tracie Austin is offering this timely book, *Alien Encounters in the Western United States*, about real encounters with what we consider extraterrestrial beings, experienced by real people. These encounters seem more convincingly authentic when accompanied by brief memories of being approached by unusual beings, discovering implanted objects in the body, noticing unusual markings on the body, having episodes of missing time, being returned to locations other than where the encounters began, and numerous other clues.

It is difficult to definitively prove that beings from other planets exist and come to earth and interact with humans, but many people who experience these episodes are convinced that they have truly had such encounters. Many people remember only the first few moments of an encounter or the last few moments, with the rest of the experience buried in their subconscious minds. Therefore, their conviction of the reality of these suspected events is enhanced by finding the details through the process of hypnotic regression.

This phenomenon of encounters with "beings from elsewhere" is gaining worldwide recognition through various media such as television specials, documentary films, radio and television interviews, internet interviews, website presentations, YouTube film clips, magazine articles, and books. An increasing number of people are expressing their belief that "we humans cannot be the only intelligent life in the entire universe," and the Vatican has announced the reality of other beings existing and coming to earth. Many highly credible witnesses are testifying to the UFOs they have seen. Countless other people are sharing their sightings of UFOs, and still others are recognizing their encounters with the occupants of UFOs.

From my longtime psychotherapy practice and my hypnosis and regression therapy practice, I am convinced that millions of people worldwide are having personal encounters with beings who are definitely "not from here." I have regressed several hundred individuals to the details of a few thousand encounter experiences, and the picture that emerges is as varied and unpredictable as it is fascinating and inspiring.

There seem to be many different types of intelligent beings who interact with us humans, and each type seems to have its own agenda with us. Some species seems to be more "self serving" and intent on using us for their purposes. Other species show much concern for humanity and the well being of the earth. Still others exude unconditional love and caring for people, take them to other dimensions for ecstatic spiritual experiences, and even do healing of serious physical problems.

Some of the encounters seem to be done astrally, with the person's mind and consciousness taken for an hour or two by the beings and then returned to the person's sleeping body. Some of the experiences seem to involve the person's whole physical body and consciousness together. Some encounters involve a massive downloading of information to the person's mind while sleeping or in an altered state of consciousness.

Other encounters seem to be with beings from other dimensions or from parallel universes. Whatever form the experiences take and with whichever beings, they deeply impact the person and alter forever his view of reality. Any "experiencer" person can have encounters with various types of beings in separate experiences. Each encounter seems to be fresh and new, different from the person's previous encounters, full of surprises, and often full of learning.

Once a person has accepted that he is having these encounters, he has the opportunity to work through his feelings and reactions. He is more likely to release his fear and become more comfortable with subsequent encounters. He may hope for close sightings of UFOs. He may even ask for additional contacts with the beings, including when he is awake and conscious.

The accounts of encounters in this book show people in different stages of realization and reactions. Blessings to these brave people for pursuing their discoveries of what they have experienced, and for sharing their awareness's with others. They help to "normalize" these kinds of experiences for others who are wondering if, or knowing that, they have these encounters as well.

Hopefully, as more of humanity awakens to the reality of our interactions with highly advanced beings, we will become more mature and cooperative among ourselves worldwide, and capable of participating intelligently and "humanely" with others in the great cosmic community.

~Barbara Lamb M.S., MFT, CHT
Certified Hypnotherapist and Regression Therapist
Author of *Alien Experiences* and *Crop Circles Revealed*
Website: www.barbaralambmft.com

Alien Encounters

"I could see two red lights coming out from the tip of this thing that did not look like a plane at all, or a helicopter. I could see a long something coming down from the center and I kept going closer and closer. I thought, 'My God, what is this thing?!' I felt myself being told to come closer and I was greatly confused by this and I blinked my eyes and I thought, 'This can't be real.' And I shook my head and turned away, and looked back and said, 'Oh, God its there. What is this thing?' I tried to put my hand toward my gun and I could not put my hand there. I cannot understand why my hands keep going up with the binoculars. I was told to keep the binoculars up and keep looking up, and keep coming closer. No harm would come to me."

~Betty and Barney Hill

Abduction Experience 1961
New Hampshire
Excerpt: *Captured – The Betty and Barney Hill UFO Experience*
by Stanton T. Friedman, MSC.,
and Kathleen Marden

Introduction

"I know this sounds crazy, but I believe I'm being visited by beings from somewhere else. I don't have any idea *who* they are, or *what* they want from me, but all I know is that they sure as hell scare me to death. I hate them, and I just want them to go away!"

These are the words from multitudes of people *worldwide* who claim that they are having physical contact with nonhuman entities – entities who they refer to as alien beings or extraterrestrials that have suddenly appeared in their lives without any form of invitation. Although sightings of UFOs have increased and gained popularity over the years, the alien encounter or abduction phenomena itself is somewhat quite different, and has always remained much more secretive than that of simply sharing a sighting of a UFO in the day or night sky.

For decades now, researchers have been investigating the UFO phenomena all across the globe, and have come to acknowledge the extraterrestrial reality and that alien encounters are indeed very real and much widespread, oftentimes becoming the main focus of the UFO subject. People from all walks of life are experiencing these strange and bizarre encounters – professional business people, police officers, students, doctors, lawyers, bankers, politicians, scientists, teachers; the list is endless. It seems that there is no specific "type" or "status" of person that these beings are choosing to interact with. Children are also having encounters with these nonhuman entities, and speak of how, sometimes, they are visited by balls of light that often enter their bedrooms. This ball of light source then interacts with the children as if playing games with them as it fly's and maneuvers around the room.

Researchers interpret this "playful" behavior to be a way of developing the child's psychic abilities, in a similar way to how a physical ball helps to develop coordination skills. Children tell of how these strange looking beings help them walk through walls, where they then find themselves onboard a spacecraft interacting and playing with children who in fact look very "different" from them, and who are typically referred to as *Hybrids*. The child often notices an entity standing off to the side watching them as they play and interact. Some children have even expressed that they learn far more from these entities onboard the craft than what they actually learn during their classes in school!

In the wonderfully written book *Abduction: Human Encounters with Aliens,* the late Dr. John E. Mack, professor of Psychiatry at Harvard Medical School, mentions that in 1987, a folklorist of the name Thomas Bullard at the University of Indiana, compiled a comprehensive guide of abductions from overseas. In it, he listed alien encounters/abductions that were reported from a number of countries. These countries included: Australia, Argentina, Bolivia, Brazil, Canada, Chile, England, Finland, France, Poland, South Africa, the Soviet Union, Spain, Uruguay, and also West Germany. He listed, however, the United States of America as the country leading the way in the number of abductions, with England and Brazil following closely behind. This could possibly be due to the fact that practicing hypnotherapists and psychotherapists in those countries have openly expressed working with abductees, helping them with the realization of and coming to terms with their bizarre and very often disturbing encounters.

The very first publication of an abduction case took place in Brazil, 1957, involving the son of a rancher, Antonio Villas Boas. To describe his encounter in brief:

> At the time of his alleged abduction, Antonio was ploughing fields at night near Sao Francisco de Sales when he saw what he described as a "red star" in the night sky. The "star" approached him growing in size until it transformed into an egg-shaped craft, with a red light at the front and a rotating device at the top.

> As the craft began to descend in the field, Antonio decided to run from the scene. His tractor failed to operate when its engine died after traveling only a short distance, and as he continued on foot, he was captured by a five-foot-tall humanoid being. Within moments, three other beings then appeared to help take him onboard their craft, where a series of bizarre and disturbing experiences transpired.

The famous case of Betty and Barney Hill's encounter and abduction occurred in 1961, while they were traveling home to New Hampshire from their Canada vacation.

Betty noticed a strange bright light in the night sky. As she observed it through binoculars, she saw a clearer image of an "odd shaped" craft with bat-like fin wings protruding from both sides of the object, and displayed flashing multicolored lights around it.

Driving further along the isolated road, the object quickly descended towards their car, where the huge, silent craft hovered above it approximately 80-100 feet before landing in front of them further ahead. Nonhuman entities approached them on the ground and walked towards the Hill's vehicle. The case unfolds as they are then taken onboard the spacecraft, where Betty is taken in one direction and Barney is led in another.

Painful and disturbing memories of these beings performing various tests on both of them during their encounter have been revealed throughout many of their hypnotic regressions.

The number of people who claim to have been abducted by occupants of UFOs has been increasing since the early 1970s, and while one gallop poll at the end of the twentieth century revealed that approximately one-third of Americans believe that aliens have visited us, another poll revealed that some four million Americans believe they've personally experienced an alien encounter – and this does not take into account the number of abductees worldwide. This is a staggering number! Could such an exponential amount of people all be prone to generating the same psychological fantasy, hallucinations, or simply lying? The answer straightforwardly, is no.

In support of this opinion are a number of well-respected and highly qualified professionals within the field of clinical psychotherapy and psychiatry, as well as regression therapy. Professionals such as the late Budd Hopkins, David Jacobs Ph.D, Yvonne Smith C.HT., Barbara Lamb MS. MFT. CHT., and the late John E. Mack M.D., to name a few, all believe that this incredibly strange phenomena is worthy of thorough examination and investigation. They consider that something very real is taking place between humans and nonhuman life forms on this planet, and in a very serious way.

Individuals like Budd Hopkins, whose book *Intruders* (1987) made it to the *New York Times* bestseller list, and eventually *Intruders*, the television mini-series (1992), explores the shocking truth about contact between humans and aliens and has played a very big part in dominating the field of Ufology, particularly that of the alien abduction scenario. Budd, and others like him in his field of expertise, have dedicated their lives to fully examining alien encounters and abductions, and although the phenomena is widespread, as previously mentioned, the abductees themselves do not always have conscious recall of their personal and disturbing encounters. These beings whoever they are, have the utmost ability to *block* or *suppress* these memories of the experience from coming to the forefront of the experiencer's mind, until perhaps some future point in time; and if or when that time arrives, the abductee may only then start to recall fragments of the experience somewhat as "dream-like," fragments which derive from residual memories of their abduction encounter.

What then typically transpires from this point forward develops into a series of flashbacks that can either appear from out of nowhere or be triggered by certain events or situations, objects, feelings, and emotions that the abductee is experiencing at that moment. Beyond the series of flashbacks, hypnosis can then be considered a powerful, and somewhat reliable, tool if used correctly for retrieving these deep hidden memories as Budd Hopkins and his fellow colleagues have demonstrated in their many years of research. It has been found that hypnosis reveals a specific pattern of action on the part of the alien beings themselves. Some experiencers, however, can fully recall their alien encounter and give a complete account with precise detail, without ever having any guidance from hypnotic regression.

How An Alien Encounter / Abduction Begins

Abduction encounters typically begin either in the person's home during the night or early hours of the morning. They can also take place while driving on a short or long journey, quite often at out-of-the-way locations, as in the case of Betty and Barney Hill's encounter.

Of the many years of research into this strange abduction phenomenon, well-respected researchers and ufologists alike know that one thing is for certain, and that is that the accounts of abductions have all displayed patterns of great similarity:

- A presence is felt in the room

- The abductee then becomes paralyzed

- They feel compelled to follow instructions from the alien being

- They are taken from their normal environment and are often floated, and then levitated, in a beam of blue light (which is the color most often reported from many witness accounts)

- There are physical examinations involved

- Telepathic communication

- Missing time

- Amnesia once the abductee/experiencer is returned home to their bed or car (wherever they were taken from)

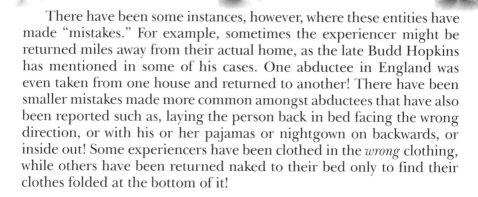

There have been some instances, however, where these entities have made "mistakes." For example, sometimes the experiencer might be returned miles away from their actual home, as the late Budd Hopkins has mentioned in some of his cases. One abductee in England was even taken from one house and returned to another! There have been smaller mistakes made more common amongst abductees that have also been reported such as, laying the person back in bed facing the wrong direction, or with his or her pajamas or nightgown on backwards, or inside out! Some experiencers have been clothed in the *wrong* clothing, while others have been returned naked to their bed only to find their clothes folded at the bottom of it!

The late Dr. John E. Mack noted in his book *Abduction: Human Encounters with Aliens*, a personal conversation that he had with Budd Hopkins some years ago. Budd told the story of a certain case of two abductees who, after an abduction, were returned to the wrong cars, and that as they drove along the highway, they recognized each other's vehicles. The beings were aware of the mistake they had made, and so the abductees were then immediately "re-abducted" and returned to their own cars!

Not Your Typical Physical Exam

Why an examination is performed is not fully understood, but is nevertheless an important part of the abduction procedure, and is extremely invasive to the experiencer. It is concluded, however, that over the many years that researchers have worked closely with abductees, they now believe that the aliens' intentions and actions have revealed their true purpose. These beings are not only performing an examination just to investigate humans and for the purpose of researching them, but evidence suggests more of an involvement in some kind of a reproductive agenda – a breeding program.

Once onboard the UFO, the person experiencing the encounter is then led by one of the beings to a certain part of the craft that is used for the sole purpose of the examination. Their clothes are removed by the beings themselves, who then telepathically ask the experiencer to lie on the table in front of them.

From a number of accounts reported over the years, some abductees have been willing to follow the aliens' requests, while others have been very reluctant to follow any of their orders at all, only to respond by showing their anger and by shouting and yelling at them. At this point, the abductee observes a taller alien being who enters the room to calm them, and who then takes control of the situation. This is done in a couple of ways: either with the being physically touching the person, or alternatively by staring closely into their eyes, where the being then uses their advanced knowledge of human physiology to control them. The abductee is then left with no choice but to engage in the stare, at which point the being telepathically tells the person that everything is okay and that they do not intend any harm. Once the situation is under control, the beings then continue with the examination procedure.

As many as five, six, or more beings have been reported to be in the room at the same time, all carrying out different tasks; some monitoring the various pieces of equipment, while others are dealing closely with the abductee, who often speaks of a light source that illuminates them on the table. Although they cannot specifically say where the light source is coming from directly, they definitely know that it's present. The table is usually metal, quite long, and similar to that of some examination tables in our own medical establishments – except that the aliens' medical table can appear to come out from the wall, or it may seem to be suspended by no physical means.

The Physical Examination

The physical examination itself consists of a myriad of tests that use various instruments to take samples from many areas of the body, including skin and hair, and those from inside the body. Some of the instruments described by the abductees are used to penetrate quite deep in many parts of their anatomy, which include the nasal cavity, the ears, and sometimes directly into the head itself, the arms, legs, feet, abdomen, and even genitalia.

But one of the most talked about and the most disturbing of procedures discussed by the abductees involves the reproductive system. During this process, they have explained how sperm samples are taken from men and ova removed from females. Many women have even experienced themselves being used as surrogate human mothers. After being impregnated with a fetus that is part extraterrestrial, within two to three months of the pregnancy, the women are then re-abducted by the beings, who then remove the fetus when it has reached a certain stage of development. The abductee sees the fetus being placed into some type of a large glass container which incubates and houses it in a propagating solution. During future abductions, the abductee often sees hybrid babies lying in incubators, ready to be raised and cared for in the alien environment.

Some experiencers have even talked about seeing small hybrid children onboard the craft, and that the aliens themselves bring a hybrid child to meet them so that the experiencer can have one-on-one time with them. In many cases, an experiencer intuitively knows that the child is their own – or the alien being tells them that this is the case. During this interaction, sometimes the abductee expresses to the being how they wish they could take the child home to love and nurture, to which the being denies their request and advises that the child could not possibly survive in the human environment.

The Beings —
We Have Cosmic Neighbors

In many of the cases reported, there are several types of beings that witnesses describe. They can be very tall humanoid-type beings with beautiful features, long or short blonde hair, often described as *Nordic* looking, and are associated with healing experiences onboard the craft. Then there are the shorter-type beings who are very dwarf-like in size, sometimes wearing hooded cloaks or robes. Others appear as small, hairy creatures with no visible signs of facial features. Still more have been reported to be insect-like, often described as looking similar to a praying mantis. Some beings have been reported as Reptilian, quite tall, and built well physically, but are rather aggressive in their nature. They also don't seem to have much regard or tolerance for the human being.

But the most common and predominant amongst the alien beings observed are the small greys, three to four feet tall and of which there are two kinds described. First, there are the small robotic, drone-type workers that have been seen both inside and outside the craft, sometimes described by the witness as "Gophers." They go for this and go for that. Second, a slightly taller grey being is noted, often referred to as the "leader" or "doctor," and felt to be male. Female leaders have also had interaction with the experiencer. They have expressed that the aliens' gender is not that obvious to them, but comes with more of an intuitive feeling that they find difficult to describe.

While some experiencers talk about their encounters being of a positive and enlightening nature, there are others who do not see it that way. For these people, they are extremely resentful of the contact and the sheer terror and emotional turmoil that these beings bring with them, and find it incredibly difficult to come to terms with.

The small greys have large pear-shaped heads that appear to be way too big for their little thin necks and bodies to support, and have long arms with three or four fingers, and very thin spindly legs. Their bodies look as though they are somewhat decomposed. They are hairless, and have little or no ears, only a thin slit for a mouth, and small holes for the nostrils. The most prominent feature that experiencers talk about is their eyes, which are huge, black, almond-shaped, and curve upward to the side of the head. The experiencer is not entirely sure whether this is some sort of a goggle or fitted eye piece covering the actual eye itself, but the eyes are most often described as having compelling power and absolute control over those looking into them. The experiencer always expresses that they desperately try to avoid looking directly into the eyes, so as not to lose their sense of will in the sheer depth of the blackness.

These beings are usually described as wearing a one piece, tight-fitting jumpsuit, so form-fitting in fact, that the abductee is not sure whether it's their own skin or a protective garment to cover it. The leader- or doctor-type alien is slightly taller, usually five feet tall and is also gray in color, whose features are much older and more wrinkled. It is obvious to the abductee that this particular entity is clearly the one in control of all procedures onboard the craft, and the abductee can often feel a strange connection to him; a connection that they have known him for all eternity, a very powerful and loving type of relationship, and one in which they feel bonded to each other. Communication with the beings is never verbal, but only that of a "telepathic" transmission, thought to thought from alien to human.

Alien Encounters

"I'm standing up on nothing. And they take me out all the way up, way above the building. Ooh, I hope I don't fall. The UFO opens up almost like a clam and then I'm inside. I see benches similar to regular benches. And they're bringing me down a hallway. Doors open like sliding doors. Inside are all these lights and buttons and a big long table. I don't want to get up on that table. They get me on the table anyway. They start saying things to me and I'm yelling. I can still yell. One of them says something that sounds like 'Nobbyegg.' I think they were trying to tell me to be quiet because he put his hand over my mouth."

~Linda Cortile

Abduction Experience 1989, New York
Excerpt: *The Manhattan Abduction*,
UFO Casebook
*Witnessed; The True Story of the
Brooklyn Bridge UFO Abductions* by Budd Hopkins

Roxanne
Meeting with an Abductee

It was in England, 1996, while organizing a UFO conference when I first met Roxanne. At that time, she was in her early twenties, single, and not really sure about which direction she was heading in her life. She was experiencing a few problems in her personal life, and, in particular, finding it difficult to sustain a usual day-to-day job – she was frequently in and out of work. Her relationship with her boyfriend was also turbulent, an "on again, off again" kind of liaison. Needless to say, she found it all a great strain and difficult to get a hold on all aspects of her life.

While most people would consider this behavior pattern to be very normal and typical of someone in their early twenties, Roxanne attributed her instability to having personally experienced alien encounters. It was immensely challenging for her to deal with "reality" or her perception of what she felt reality should be, and that encounters with the unknown had disrupted her life in a big way.

She had contacted me not only to share her stories of personal UFO sightings, but more importantly because of her frightening encounters with the alien beings themselves. We had initially agreed to meet for lunch one afternoon, and during our lengthy conversation, Roxanne revealed to me how her encounters first began. Of course, like many abductees, she felt that it was extremely difficult to talk about her experiences so openly with just anyone, and made a point of mentioning that, because of my involvement with the UFO subject, she wanted to reach out to me, and trusted that I would believe her experiences wholeheartedly – and I did.

At a very young age of around two or three years old, Roxanne remembered seeing "strange people" around her play pen, and as many as three or four of them at a time. They would just appear from out of the wall, gather together and simply observe her. This would happen frequently, and it wasn't until she was much older and upon reflection of her life that she remembered other hints of encounters, and started to fit pieces of the puzzle together to realize that these "strange people" had played a big part in her life as she was growing up.

Roxanne was emotional about remembering a number of bizarre incidents that happened throughout her childhood, and explained that they were weird and never made any sense to her. According to many documented accounts from witnesses, alien/human interaction during childhood does appear to be the general rule to the UFO/ alien phenomenon. Various reports do indicate that these experiences start from as early as the cradle and continue to the grave. In some circumstances, these alien beings do, in fact, interact with a person throughout their whole life.

Another interesting point is that these beings are highly interested in family genetics and family lineage. For example, if *you* are an abductee, it's likely that your mother has also had some interaction with these entities, and that her mother has also experienced them during her life. There's a generational theme occurring and is of great importance to these beings. This scenario also seemed to be the case with Roxanne and her mother's side of the family, although her mother was not really open to discussing any of her experiences with anyone at that time.

Roxanne described an event to me that transpired one night, an experience that involved a UFO sighting late at night over a large wooded area where she lived, known as Hanchurch Woods. Hanchurch Woods is located in the West Midlands area. It's a private estate which is close to the towns of Newcastle-under-Lyme and Stoke-on-Trent, and has a thousand acres of forestry. I knew the area quite well, as I lived close by the location myself, and so was familiar with the area to which she was referring.

On this particular night and while at home, she happened to notice a "star" that moved slowly at first across the sky, which then gained speed and momentum and became very erratic in its movement. At this point, Roxanne knew that it was definitely not a star, nor a helicopter, plane, or any other kind of conventional type of aircraft, for that matter. She said:

> It was just too weird to be anything related to normal aircraft, and was silent; the aerodynamics were just so different and strange.

None of her family was home at the time and so she witnessed the entire event by herself – or so she thought.

After a few hours had lapsed from initially observing the object, which stayed in sight for approximately twenty to twenty-five minutes or so, and although Roxanne was intrigued by what she had seen, she thought nothing more of the sighting and went to bed. Upon awakening the following morning, she felt somewhat unnerved and shaken by a "dream" that she'd had that the previous night. In this "dream" she found herself onboard a craft, and in a room that had a sterile and medical feel to it – a very ominous-looking room – and surrounded by a number of four-foot-tall, gray-looking entities, all with large heads, very thin bodies, and huge black eyes.

She mentioned that two of them were immediately close to her as she lay on some type of examining table, with one alien being at her feet, and the other standing closely behind her head. The others were all moving around the room working with various pieces of equipment. Although she couldn't specifically recall what medical procedures were done to her and was somewhat vague about the examination, what she did remember is that a being approached her from the right-hand side of the table holding what looked like a hybrid baby in its arms, and telepathically suggested to her that this baby was hers. The being made it very clear to Roxanne that it wanted her to hold the baby, to bring it close, love, and nurture it.

Roxanne knew that it was no "ordinary" baby. It didn't look human, other than having two arms and legs, but the head was unusually large for the baby's size and with large eyes. Roxanne, scared of what was presented to her, pushed herself up off the table, and with her hands outstretched in front of her made a backing-off gesture and said out loud to the being that she didn't want to hold the baby under any circumstances. She was terrified of it.

Thinking back on this now, I can understand how anyone might think that Roxanne had dreamt the whole situation due to the fact she'd witnessed the UFO the night before. But this is not the case, as I will discuss a little further in the chapter.

I suggested exploring the possibility of hypnotherapy to her as a tool of bringing the subconscious memories forward, as only certain fragments of the experience were remembered, and also that she did not recall the specifics of entering or coming back from the craft. Unfortunately, she declined to participate with any regression therapy at the time due to fear of the unknown, and wasn't prepared to accept the reality of knowing what had truly happened to her once having gone through the motions of hypnosis and discovering the truth. She simply wasn't ready, and so I supported her decision to not go through with it.

However, in the meantime, I thought it would be beneficial for her to draw what she remembered while onboard the craft, and once she did, Roxanne had a revelation and made the statement that she felt the whole process to be extremely therapeutic for her.

Approximately two weeks later, Roxanne called me and asked if she could meet with me again as she had something very important and disturbing to tell me. During a routine check up at the dentist's office, a number of x-rays were taken of Roxanne's upper and lower teeth. Upon the dentist reviewing these x-rays, he noticed a half-inch-long dark metallic object embedded in the upper left side of her jaw. He asked her about it, asking if she knew what it was and if she might have gotten something lodged in her jaw, or perhaps had fallen with something becoming embedded. Roxanne replied *no* to both questions. They were both truly dumbfounded as to what this object could be, and the dentist commented that he had never seen anything like it before in all his years of dental practice.

I had my own thoughts as to what this strange object was, having been involved with researching the subject for almost a decade. I had heard and read about many cases where abductees had discovered these strange-looking dark gray, metallic objects – or implants as they are commonly referred to – in various parts of their bodies, and sometimes the physiological feelings that some people were having from them.

When I asked Roxanne what her thoughts about the object were, she responded immediately by saying that she felt it was some kind of an "information chip." She definitely felt she was being monitored in some way by the alien beings, and that through the device, they were somehow tracking her, similar to how we track animals with various devices.

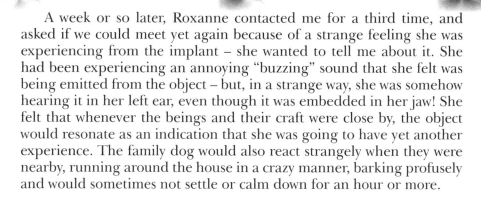

A week or so later, Roxanne contacted me for a third time, and asked if we could meet yet again because of a strange feeling she was experiencing from the implant – she wanted to tell me about it. She had been experiencing an annoying "buzzing" sound that she felt was being emitted from the object – but, in a strange way, she was somehow hearing it in her left ear, even though it was embedded in her jaw! She felt that whenever the beings and their craft were close by, the object would resonate as an indication that she was going to have yet another experience. The family dog would also react strangely when they were nearby, running around the house in a crazy manner, barking profusely and would sometimes not settle or calm down for an hour or more.

I asked Roxanne what she thought about having the object removed. I told her that I would inquire with my own dentist to see if he would remove the object privately, and that I would cover the cost for her. But, not surprising to me, she felt that she should not remove the object, even though she was experiencing sheer frustration from the buzzing effects of it.

Roxanne's case is a typical one that showed all the signs of some kind of mind control from the beings themselves, and how they are able to control and manipulate a person's thoughts – they very much control a situation for their *own* benefit.

This is just one of many accounts that you will read about in this book where the abductee suddenly feels that they should leave the object in the body, as this feels to be the right thing to do.

Roxanne's Alien Encounter Onboard The Craft

Alien Encounters

"I looked past the upper edge of the device. I could see the blurry figures of the doctors, leaning over me with their white masks and caps. They were wearing unusual, orange-colored surgical gowns. I could not make out their faces clearly. Abruptly my vision cleared. The sudden horror of what I saw rocked me as I realized that I was definitely not in a hospital. I was looking squarely into the face of a horrible creature! It looked steadily back at me with huge, luminous brown eyes the size of quarters."

~Travis Walton

Abduction Experience
1975, Arizona
Exerpt from
The Walton Experience – The Aliens

Dina's Encounter
Las Vegas, Nevada

Experiencer/Abductee

Consciously, Dina was aware of having visitations from nonhuman entities since she was five years old. They would initially come through the closed bedroom window, or appear from out of the closet; and sometimes, they would just appear in the corner of her room. As many as two or three beings would show up during any visitation.

At first, she referred to them as "Leprechauns," as being so young she didn't know *what* to call them, and sometimes would tell her parents that "Casper the Ghost" was in her room. But it wasn't until later, growing up, that Dina came to realize that these strange-looking beings were, in fact, the typical grey-type entities that many abductees are so familiar with.

As a child, Dina was always terrified of them, and every night while going to bed, it was a constant ritual for her to make sure that the night lights were switched on, that the closet door was securely shut, that the door from the bedroom to the hallway was ajar, that the drapes to the window were completely closed, and that she had a flashlight with her at all times within easy reach while she slept. She was always very afraid of the dark, and oftentimes found it difficult to sleep because of the possibility that the visitors, once again, decided to show up. Sometimes, she would even sleep underneath the bed, or on top of it with all of her stuffed animals and toys on top of her so that they wouldn't find her. But tricking them never really worked; they would find her no matter where she was sleeping.

Telepathically they would ask her not to be afraid, and she remembers how they would take her by levitating her out of the bed, placing her in some kind of a transparent "bubble-like" device that would then float through the house, past her sleeping parents who she could see sleeping in their bed, then up through the ceiling, through the roof, and up-up-up into the sky. This was a recurring ordeal for Dina, so much so that she was

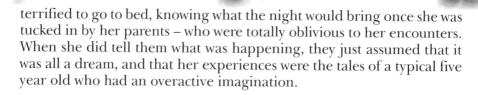

terrified to go to bed, knowing what the night would bring once she was tucked in by her parents – who were totally oblivious to her encounters. When she did tell them what was happening, they just assumed that it was all a dream, and that her experiences were the tales of a typical five year old who had an overactive imagination.

During the 1980s, Dina had a fascination with a little character on the front of a "Mr. Salty" pretzel box, and would cut out every single character from every box that was brought into the house to collect and to play with. These characters strangely reminded her of the beings that would appear in her room. One day, Dina showed these little cardboard figures to her parents and told them that the strange people she would see in her room looked like them. But again, her parents didn't take her experiences seriously.

There were many nights as a child that she would see two to three owls floating outside her window, silently, and would never dare to open the window because of them. Coincidentally, her Grandmother had a fascination with owls, and would collect everything in sight – pictures of owls, small owl figurines, owl wind chimes, and she had a cabinet full of owl collectibles. When trips were arranged for Dina to visit her Grandmother's house, Dina never really wanted to go and didn't look forward to it. This was because the owls her Grandmother collected reminded her of those she had been seeing outside her bedroom window, that always terrified her so much.

At the age of eleven, Dina's fear of the dark was still prevalent, and at one time, her father took her to see a psychiatrist to help with this phobia that she always carried with her. But while going through the motions of the psychiatrist having her sit in the dark, Dina became quite ill. She began to vomit intensely as she recalled a memory from her subconscious of one of her alien encounters. The beings had placed her in some type of an isolation tank that was completely dark. She remembered that she would be placed in this tank if she did not comply with what they were asking her to do, and most especially if she had put up any kind of a resistance with them. In this tank was complete silence and absolute stillness.

Today, she remembers that it was one of the worst feelings ever, and such a terrifying experience that she will never forget it. On the craft, the beings wanted Dina to interact with them; she would have to guess what object they were thinking of and to either point to it on a screen, or draw it. If she was correct, she would be rewarded, and if not, she

was put inside the isolation tank. Dina was also forced to look at a large screen that showed various images of mass destruction on Earth, and noticed that the beings would watch her closely to see her emotions and reactions as she continued to look on.

The childhood encounters were not only isolated to Dina, however. Her younger brother also had encounters with beings, and in particular, an entity that he called a "paper witch," that absolutely terrified him. He would also see it floating outside his bedroom window. On some occasions, he would actually see it standing in his bedroom. He was so frightened of it that he would never talk about it, and because of this experience, celebrating Halloween was never fun, as it always created such deep anxiety for him. So anything to do with witches was completely forbidden in the house.

As he got older, he turned to religion in a very serious way, and became a devout born-again Christian. For Dina to have any kind of conversation with him about their childhood encounters was completely off limits, as his view of the entire experiences were all the signs of being demonic in his viewpoint. For Dina, however, she didn't see it that way. To her, they were undoubtedly extraterrestrial visitations.

As she reached puberty, her encounters changed and became much more involved. At the age of sixteen, she would frequently be taken onboard the aliens' vessel and shown a certain part of it, where she would see many babies in their early stages of fetal development. The babies would be floating in what appeared to be glass-like cylinders, all lined up in a row, approximately two and a half feet long, and suspended in a bubbling-reddish liquid. Dina was of the impression that once these babies had reached a certain stage of their development, they would then be taken from the cylinders and placed in some type of an incubator, or box-type drawer.

Dina remembers that there were many of these "drawers" that were placed inside a long wall that displayed ambient lighting from behind it, and noticed that the temperature in this "incubatorium" was quite hot. Every drawer contained a baby, and she guessed that there were approximately thirty babies in total, and that they didn't look human. They were very small, thin, and very sickly looking with no hair, and their eyes were completely closed. Their skin was a pinkish-brown color that was clammy to the touch.

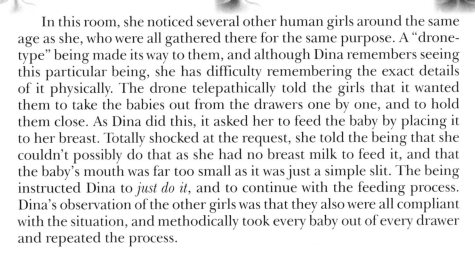

In this room, she noticed several other human girls around the same age as she, who were all gathered there for the same purpose. A "drone-type" being made its way to them, and although Dina remembers seeing this particular being, she has difficulty remembering the exact details of it physically. The drone telepathically told the girls that it wanted them to take the babies out from the drawers one by one, and to hold them close. As Dina did this, it asked her to feed the baby by placing it to her breast. Totally shocked at the request, she told the being that she couldn't possibly do that as she had no breast milk to feed it, and that the baby's mouth was far too small as it was just a simple slit. The being instructed Dina to *just do it*, and to continue with the feeding process. Dina's observation of the other girls was that they also were all compliant with the situation, and methodically took every baby out of every drawer and repeated the process.

It was here, at this incubatorium, that Dina recalls seeing a tall Reptilian being wearing a cloak, and was of the impression that he was supervising the situation, making sure that everything was operating smoothly. She compared him to looking slightly similar to that of a dinosaur due to the elongated face and scales on his skin, and although he was scary to look at, she didn't know if he was, in fact, malevolent or not. It was only during this one occasion that Dina had seen such a being as this.

In another encounter, when Dina was of the same age, she remembered being taken onboard the craft and lying on an examining table. This table had a surface that was similar to memory foam, in that it molded itself to the body and gave a feeling of "sucking" you into place. She couldn't move whatsoever. A few beings made their way around the table, a taller being accompanied by a couple of smaller gray ones. Dina knew that some procedure was about to take place, and began to feel agitated and annoyed at not being able to move. One of the grey beings began to stare deeply into Dina's eyes to both calm and quiet her, and telepathically it told her that everything was going to be fine.

The taller being had some type of a shield or cover over his face. Dina was of the impression that this being was almost human due to the appearance of his body, but she could not make out any facial features because of the shield or mask that was covering it. She watched as he took a long metal type device and inserted it through her naval. The pain was unbelievably excruciating, and Dina screamed and shouted out for them to stop. At that moment, one of the beings continued to tell her to be quiet and that the procedure would not take long. The so-called "procedure" was to take ova from Dina's ovaries.

Interestingly enough, when Dina experienced her first gynecological examination at the age of sixteen because of an infection, the doctor became curious about her sexual activities. He asked her at what age she first had sexual intercourse, as he was of the opinion from the examination that she was no longer a virgin. Dina, completely taken aback and insulted by the comment, vehemently denied what the doctor was suggesting, and told him that she had never engaged in any sexual activity whatsoever, and that she was just not interested in sex.

The doctor didn't believe Dina's claims, and took the matter in his own hands by confronting her mother who was sitting in the waiting room, and proceeded to tell her about what he had discovered during the exam. Dina was completely embarrassed by the Doctor's confrontation with her mother, and to make matters worse, her mother believed him and was convinced that Dina was lying. As a result of the Doctor's speculation, her mother was intent on having her daughter now take some form of birth control which Dina objected to, but was forced to anyway. Totally upset by the whole situation, she still denied to her mother ever engaging in any sexual activities – her mother still refused to believe her.

During 1996, Dina decided to try a hypnotherapy session for a second time, as she was still experiencing fear of the dark. However, the regression was not as successful as Dina had hoped, as her fear was not cured. But what did transpire during the regression was a memory of one of her past alien encounters and of being onboard a UFO. In particular, the "baby feeding" experience in the incubatorium came forward.

A couple of years later, in 1998, now married and in her late thirties, Dina arranged another gynecological appointment. This time, to change from her usual method of birth control to an Intra Uterine Device, as the previous form of contraception was creating a number of health issues. During the examination itself, the doctor informed Dina that the procedure wouldn't take too long, and should be fairly simple due to the fact of her already having had several children. Interestingly, Dina had never had any children, and was stunned at the doctor's presumption. He, in turn, was surprised at Dina's response to never having had children, as to him, the examination proved the contrary.

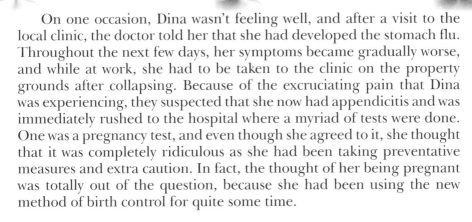

On one occasion, Dina wasn't feeling well, and after a visit to the local clinic, the doctor told her that she had developed the stomach flu. Throughout the next few days, her symptoms became gradually worse, and while at work, she had to be taken to the clinic on the property grounds after collapsing. Because of the excruciating pain that Dina was experiencing, they suspected that she now had appendicitis and was immediately rushed to the hospital where a myriad of tests were done. One was a pregnancy test, and even though she agreed to it, she thought that it was completely ridiculous as she had been taking preventative measures and extra caution. In fact, the thought of her being pregnant was totally out of the question, because she had been using the new method of birth control for quite some time.

The results of the pregnancy test came back positive, and Dina was utterly shocked at the news. She thought that there must have been some big mistake; she couldn't possibly be pregnant – there was just no way. The next thing Dina knew, she was being taken to the operating room where the doctors preformed an inner uterine sonogram to locate the Intra Uterine Device. Initially, there was some difficulty trying to locate it with the sonogram, and it took some time before it was detected. Strangely enough, the device was deeply embedded and very high up inside the wall of Dina's uterus, and was pushed to the right side.

The pregnancy turned out to be an ectopic one, as the fetus was developing in her right ovary. The five weeks of pregnancy had resulted in the ovary becoming very large and strained, eventually rupturing very badly. The doctor removed the remains of Dina's right ovary, and the Intra Uterine Device had to be cut from the area where it was deeply embedded. Throughout the entire five weeks of Dina being unaware of her pregnancy, she never once felt any symptoms, never gaining an ounce of weight, or experiencing any other bodily changes – nor did she have any morning sickness whatsoever.

The doctor commented to Dina that this was one of the most bizarre birth control incidents he had ever seen, with such a device as this. He made a point of telling her that he was going to note this in his *Journal of Obstetrics* for future reference, as it was a very unusual case. An ectopic pregnancy is one in which the pregnancy implants itself outside the uterine cavity, and with rare exceptions are not viable. They are potentially a medical emergency, and if not treated properly can result in death.

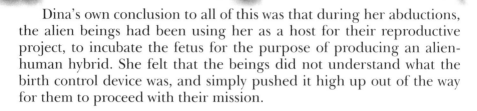

Dina's own conclusion to all of this was that during her abductions, the alien beings had been using her as a host for their reproductive project, to incubate the fetus for the purpose of producing an alien-human hybrid. She felt that the beings did not understand what the birth control device was, and simply pushed it high up out of the way for them to proceed with their mission.

Dina's case is not an isolated one by any means. There are a number of accounts where many other women have reported a similar scenario, in that they are being used as a surrogate mother or human host. It's recognized from many years of research of women from all over the world who have had these encounters. The evidence strongly suggests that the alien procedures are a process of their reproductive agenda. Researchers are aware that these entities are taking human ova and sperm which are then fertilized in vitro.

The second stage is to add their own alien genetic material to it and then to place the hybrid embryo in utero. It's stated in Dr. Jacob's book, *The Threat*, that this scenario is the same for women who were either postmenopausal or who have had hysterectomies. The fetus would be contained in some form of a sack acting as an artificial womb environment within the female, that provides the fetus with all the nourishment it needs. Within a couple of months or so, the beings actually remove the fetus and the sack, completely extracting everything. These women are still used as a human host regardless, and conclude that the alien agenda is one that is totally self-serving.

Over the years, Dina has also experienced these beings placing small objects in various areas of her body. One was embedded in her nasal cavity. It was a round object, gray in color, and the size of a small "BB," but shaped similar to that of a pomegranate seed, and was attached to the septum. Dina had no idea how long this object had been there, and only noticed it one day when her husband had brought her a magnifying make-up mirror. As she was applying her make-up, she tilted her head upwards which revealed the object at a closer angle.

Dina doesn't consciously remember this object being placed in her nasal cavity during her encounters on the craft, but in so many abduction cases, the experiencer is blocked from remembering the procedure, as typically these beings do not want the objects removed. But this is exactly what Dina did. She visited an eye, nose, and throat (ENT) doctor who removed the strange-looking object from her nose, and placed it in a small vile. He had no idea what the object could possibly be, as he had never seen anything like it before. He asked Dina if she could take it to the Lab as it was in the same building and only a few floors below his office. She complied and watched one of the medical staff attach a label to the vile and write Dina's full name on it.

A week later, she had not heard any news from the laboratory and so followed up with a phone call. Interestingly, none of the medical staff had any idea of what Dina was talking about. They searched thoroughly through their medical records but found nothing. She reiterated her full name again to the person on the phone, and the exact date she had dropped the specimen off. She also gave the name of the doctor who had removed it, but they still couldn't recall it. What was also strange about this was that Dina never received a bill for the lab test, and today still finds it difficult to come up with an explanation for the disappearance of the object.

Another one of these strange objects was located behind Dina's left knee, which she believes to have just disappeared on its own accord, or either removed during one of her encounters on the craft. She also found yet another small object on her left shin, which was removed by a dermatologist who thought the object to be very bizarre. It was round, and had some kind of a "tether" attached to it which Dina could move all the way around her shin area.

Additionally, there is a noticeable object protruding from under the skin behind Dina's left ear, and on the occasion will hear a "buzzing" sound coming from it. One day she happened to show the object to a friend, but as she did, it seemed to suck itself back into place so that her friend was unable to touch it. Dina still has it behind her left ear to this present day.

Alien Encounters

"There was no mistake it was coming directly to us. Then I remember standing on the lakeshore watching the object hovering above the lake 50 to 75 yards in front of us... Then the search beam went upward into the sky and we saw it moving away at a tremendous speed. We all seemed to be in a state of shock... We just stood there unable to talk or move."

~Jim Weiner

Abduction Experience 1976, Maine
Excerpt: *The Allagash Abductions*
UFOevidence.org

Ron's Encounter
Utah

Experiencer/Abductee

Ron has experienced contact with extraterrestrials for forty-three years of his life, beginning when he was fourteen years old. Many of his alien encounters have been very intense, extremely personal, and too numerous to detail individually, but nevertheless, each experience in this chapter has been chosen for its remarkable content and for its validity of alien contact. Ron's experiences have included many conscious encounters of physically being onboard the craft, interacting with the alien beings themselves, and seeing their alien system of alphabetic symbols of which he has been taught – not to mention physical marks and scars on his body, and an implant that remains behind his left ear. Here are various accounts of Ron's Alien Encounters.

In August 1967, Ron was invited to visit his uncle's horse ranch in the countryside just outside of Riverside, California, where his uncle raised thoroughbred horses. At the time, Ron was taking a summer vacation from school and his Uncle thought it would be a good idea for him to help out at the ranch, and in particular helping to replace a water line that led from the highway to the house. So, after getting permission from his parents, Ron made the trip to visit his uncle. It was here that Ron's alien contact first began.

The usual daily routine on the ranch started fairly early in the morning and ended approximately 3.30 p.m., as the outdoor temperatures were quite unbearable at that time of the year, usually in the triple digits. It was now the third night of Ron's visit, and after finishing the days chores on the ranch, Ron, his uncle, and his aunt sat and relaxed for awhile watching television, ate dinner and made pleasant conversation, until around 10 p.m. or so, when Ron decided to go to bed as the days activities had been totally exhausting. At approximately midnight, "something" woke Ron from a deep sleep and he immediately felt a presence in the room.

Lying in bed and too terrified to look at first, from his peripheral view, he could see a greenish glow manifesting in one corner of the room, where within moments a tall being materialized standing in the corner observing him. Now turning his head fully to look, Ron saw that the being was approximately seven and a half feet tall, its head only a few inches from the ceiling. He was grayish white in color, with a large bald head and an extremely anorexic looking body, where Ron could see the ribs protruding out from under the skin. The being also had very large black round eyes (not the typical large almond shape more commonly seen with grey entities), sunken cheeks, somewhat of a pointed chin, unusually long arms, and three long fingers and a thumb on each hand.

Throughout the whole time of the being's presence, Ron could hear a series of mechanical "clicking" sounds, approximately every minute or so, which went on for quite some time. Absolutely terrified, Ron closed his eyes tightly and prayed to God for the being to disappear. He had no idea how long he lay there with his eyes closed, but eventually, when he did open them, the being had disappeared. The strange "clicking" sound, however, remained for a few hours afterward.

A day or so after this experience, Ron began having a series of "dreams" of being in a strange, white and brightly lit room that had a table in the middle of it. He would notice that the same seven-foot-tall being would be present on the occasion, but also, always present and lying on the table, would be a six-foot-tall strange-looking entity that appeared to be more like that of a mannequin or a doll, with a bumpy hairless head and large, black shiny-round eyes. The tall being standing in the corner of the room would telepathically tell Ron to climb up on the table and to begin having intercourse with the entity.

Ron who was only fourteen at the time had no idea what was going on or why the being was asking him to do this. He felt extremely awkward at the request, but also felt that the tall being observing him had total control over his actions at all times, and could do nothing but comply with what the being had asked him to do. During the sexual encounter, there was no reaction whatsoever from the entity laying on the table, "she" was totally motionless and Ron felt that she wasn't real. After many repeated sexual experiences with this entity, everything in the room would then suddenly turn a fuzzy white, and Ron would find himself back in bed.

After many years of this strange and difficult-to-understand experience, *and* not being able to tell a soul about it, Ron, in hindsight,

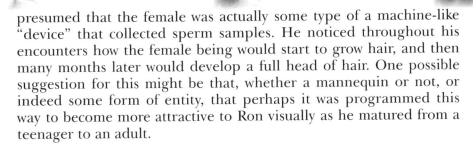

presumed that the female was actually some type of a machine-like "device" that collected sperm samples. He noticed throughout his encounters how the female being would start to grow hair, and then many months later would develop a full head of hair. One possible suggestion for this might be that, whether a mannequin or not, or indeed some form of entity, that perhaps it was programmed this way to become more attractive to Ron visually as he matured from a teenager to an adult.

After every encounter with this being, there would be a lime-green-colored substance both on Ron's body and underwear. Feeling too embarrassed to place the underwear in the laundry, Ron would quietly creep outside the house, so as to not awaken his parents, and throw his underwear to the bottom of the trash. This sexual encounter would happen once every two weeks, and continued repeatedly until Ron was approximately thirty years old, when it then abruptly stopped.

Beyond these sexual experiences onboard the craft, Ron repeatedly witnessed numerous UFO sightings and encountered alien visitations at his home. He would also experience visitations from animals, an owl in particular, that would sit perched on the front porch of his mother's house, and remain there constantly day and night for over a week. Every morning, the owl would watch him walk down the steps to get into his truck to go to work, and when Ron returned home, the owl would still be perched in the same spot, watching him get out of the truck, walk up the steps, and go into the house. Every day was the same.

Another instance that Ron recalls, was of having a visit from a deer shortly after a UFO sighting in 1971.

During that time, Ron had moved to Wyoming. Here he would physically see UFOs on many occasions before having his encounters. He had just graduated from high school, and landed a job in Grand Teton National Park. The summer job was temporary, three months in all, but he would make regular visits to his parents in Utah every other weekend. During a Sunday afternoon in August after visiting his parents, Ron headed back to his job at the National Park. After arriving in Wyoming somewhere between 11:30 p.m. and midnight, he stopped at a gas station to fill up his truck and to get a snack. He then headed North, where he approached a crossroads and crested a hill.

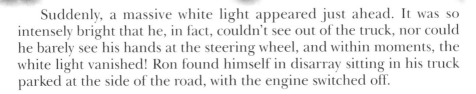

Suddenly, a massive white light appeared just ahead. It was so intensely bright that he, in fact, couldn't see out of the truck, nor could he barely see his hands at the steering wheel, and within moments, the white light vanished! Ron found himself in disarray sitting in his truck parked at the side of the road, with the engine switched off.

Ron showed up late to work later that morning. The drive itself was only 170 miles from where the experience had occurred, but had taken between seven to eight hours to drive that particular distance. Undoubtedly, Ron had experienced a tremendous amount of missing time.

The very next night after the incident, Ron was awakened by "something" between the hours of 2:30 a.m. and 3 a.m. There was a loud noise at the door. Ron got out of bed to investigate the noise, and upon opening the door, saw an extremely strange sight. A deer stood in front of him. They both stared at each other for quite sometime. What's strange about this encounter is that the deer was standing inside the building! There was no access to the outside from where Ron was sleeping, as he was staying in a dormitory at the time, and all of the rooms were enclosed.

The use of animals and images of animals plays quite a large role in the abduction phenomena, and are used, it seems, as some kind of a "screen memory" by alien beings to block out actual encounters, and to make the experiencer feel less fearful by presenting a memory of an animal – either an owl or a deer, instead of the alien being itself. Why specifically an owl or a deer is not known.

Some years later, Ron had regression therapy to uncover the missing time of the bright-light incident. The regression revealed that Ron had initially seen the bright flash of light and recalled his vehicle being parked at the side of the road – except that Ron was not in his vehicle, but standing on top of the hill by a barbed-wire fence, next to a large pasture. He remembered that there was a dirt road across the way that led down the hill for a quarter of a mile, and at the end of the dirt road was a house with its lights switched on, and a large barn next door to it. For some reason, Ron had suggested in the regression that the house and the barn had also been involved in the encounter, but could not specifically say how.

Still under regression, Ron looked down the hill towards his truck. He recalled seeing a large, white and brightly lit "cloud" over his truck that illuminated the entire surroundings, and sticking out from the top of this cloud, Ron could see what appeared to be a circular craft that had a row of rectangular windows around it. At that point, Ron's memory was completely blocked, and he could go no further with the regression. What later transpired after the regression therapy, was a series of reoccurring dreams that continued for a number of years afterward.

The "Dream"

The dream always began with Ron walking up a stairway that lead to a large, round building that floated twenty to twenty-five feet off the ground. Ron noticed the trees and shrubs underneath it as he climbed the stairs. The building was shaped like a doughnut, and had very large windows that were approximately ten feet apart. The windows had beams situated in the center area that ran down between each individual window and through the floor. Inside the craft, he noticed people lying around unconscious – men, women, children, some naked, others wearing clothes, and people of many different races and nationalities. He sensed his fear and anxiety as he slowly walked down a narrow hallway that had doors on both sides. The hallway was approximately thirty feet long, and the last door on the left was partially opened. Ron hesitated as he approached it.

He immediately felt that he had to get out of this place, and started running past the door, turning to look inside as he ran by. He saw someone inside the room lying on a table, or what looked to be more like a gurney. He continued to run, turning right down the hallway, and right again which lead to a dead end. He noticed a door on the left and opened it to walk inside. It was a very small room, approximately twenty-by-twenty feet long, with an armless chair in the middle of it sitting on a pedestal. In front of the chair was something resembling a chalk board. Ron immediately felt his anxiety growing more and more intense, and left the room running back to where he'd started. After some time of running further down the hallway, backwards and forwards around the doughnut-shaped building to find his way out, he eventually saw the stairs. As he got to the bottom of them, he would suddenly wake up.

For many years, the dream always appeared exactly the same, except for the very last time when Ron made the decision to enter the door where he'd noticed someone lying on the gurney.

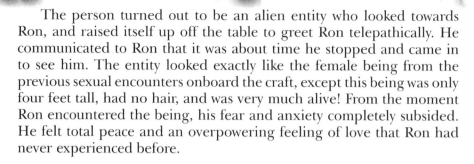

The person turned out to be an alien entity who looked towards Ron, and raised itself up off the table to greet Ron telepathically. He communicated to Ron that it was about time he stopped and came in to see him. The entity looked exactly like the female being from the previous sexual encounters onboard the craft, except this being was only four feet tall, had no hair, and was very much alive! From the moment Ron encountered the being, his fear and anxiety completely subsided. He felt total peace and an overpowering feeling of love that Ron had never experienced before.

The being was male, with an odd lumpiness to the head, large black eyes, and skin that was an off-white to a very light beige in color, with three very long fingers and a thumb. The being came face-to-face with Ron, and remained silent. Ron felt that the being was downloading a tremendous amount of information into his brain. After a while, the being lay back down on the table and telepathically told Ron that it was now time for him to leave, but that they would be seeing each other again in the near future. He expressed to Ron that he did not want him to worry or panic about his encounter, and neither to be fearful of it. After meeting with the being, Ron was left with a feeling of total awe from the entity's presence.

As Ron left the room, he continued on down the hallway and up a flight of steps where he could see the other people lying unconscious. He had a deep knowing that they were all going to be fine, and that they were not going to be harmed in any way.

This particular dream was the final one of it's kind for Ron.

In 1986, Ron had yet another encounter with a deer, after purchasing a trailer house in Utah. One evening, shortly after Ron went to bed, he began to feel paralyzed and felt that another encounter was about to begin. Ron tried to fight the feeling of it immediately, but could not. Suddenly, the blankets started to levitate and move off the bed.

The very next thing that Ron remembered was that he was being dropped from a height onto the coffee table in the living room, smashing down onto it extremely hard and breaking all of its legs in the process. He had no idea how this could have happened, as one minute he was lying in bed trying to fall asleep, and the next he was being transported unconsciously into a different area of the house. Totally bewildered by what had just transpired, Ron then heard a noise at the back door. He opened it only to find a deer standing in front of him. The porch itself was totally enclosed, and Ron had no idea how the animal could have even got in.

They stood there staring at each other for quite some time, and after a while, the deer slowly backed away, watching Ron as he continued to walk backwards down the steps, turning its body as it reached the bottom step to walk away, but continuing to stare at Ron as he did so. With so many bizarre encounters occurring throughout Ron's life, he feels certain that the deer was, in fact, an alien entity that had morphed into the animal, possibly so as to not scare Ron after just having had the strange experience inside the house.

Another encounter happened in June 1997 when Ron had moved to Hawaii, where he had taken a job in construction. His boss had planned a party one night at his home and Ron attended. Many people showed up at the house and everyone was having an enjoyable evening, eating great food and having wonderful conversation. At 11 p.m. or so, Ron decided to leave the party as the next day was a working day for him, even though it happened to be a weekend. On the way home, Ron took a back road that led directly to his house, rather than taking the busy freeway.

Only a few miles away from reaching his home, Ron noticed a "walnut-shaped" light that appeared above the mountains. As Ron looked on, he realized that the light was quite huge in size, and pulled over to get out of his truck for a better look. Suddenly, the light started to move upwards through the clouds, moving up higher and higher before eventually blinking out. Within moments, he noticed that the light reappeared further over the mountains and started to move erratically, making zig-zag movements before moving closer and heading towards Ron's direction.

He now became fearful as the object came closer. He watched it as it remained in close proximity for sometime before it moved back over the mountains. After a while, Ron decided to make his way home again. The sighting was still on his mind the whole time, and as he reached the driveway, his curiosity got the better of him. He thought that he might be able to see the object again from the back of the house. He waited and waited, but nothing.

Later that night, as Ron went to bed, within moments he felt his body becoming totally paralyzed. Now, only able to move his eyes, he could see the blankets slowly levitating off the bed and falling onto the floor. Suddenly, six grey beings appeared and came in from the direction of the bedroom door. The beings stood watching Ron for a few moments. He noticed that these beings were a little different from the usual grey-type entities, as their heads were a very light blue in color, but yet gray from the neck downwards. A thought crossed his mind that perhaps they were all wearing some kind of a tight fitting jump suit.

Ron now felt his body levitating off the bed. He tried to scream and force himself to move physically, but could not. Powerless, he levitated horizontally towards the bedroom door and out into the living room, where the entities formed themselves in a group of three on either side of him. He levitated past the kitchen and into the foyer of the house and physically passed through the closed front door. Now outside by the palm trees in the drive way, he could see straight up into the night sky, where the walnut-shaped craft he had seen earlier awaited his arrival. A dull beam of light came down from the object which then levitated Ron vertically up into the waiting UFO. His body became very sensitive in the light and he felt a strange buzzing sensation as he slowly moved up with the beam. Ron recalled it being an extremely odd feeling, and was very fearful of heights. He quickly became concerned that he might actually fall once he got above the rooftop of his house.

Still traveling upwards, he could see the top of the neighbors' houses, and looking down, he could see his truck in the driveway and the six entities on the ground watching him as he approached the craft. Entering the bottom of it, he found himself inside a white, hazy room and lying on a table. Three grey beings stood on each side of him, staring. No communication was given. Ron tried to yell and move his body, when all of a sudden, he heard a loud "bang" and found himself hitting the floor next to his bed, and totally naked. Shocked by what had just happened, and dripping in sweat, he looked around the room, and saw his clothes on the bed and the pillow at the foot of it.

Wondering what had just happened to him, he got up off the floor and made his way to the bathroom to take a shower. The experience kept playing over and over in Ron's mind. Now 4 a.m., he got back into bed. No sooner he did, than his body once again started to become paralyzed. He immediately tried to move his body and tried to scream but without any success. Then again he found himself back in the hazy, white-lit room. But this time without any entities present. Within a few moments, he heard the loud "bang" sound again, and found himself back in his bedroom by the side of the bed. Now 6:45 a.m., Ron realized that he had almost three hours of missing time. Once again he showered, and prepared himself to go to work that morning.

This was yet another very strange encounter for Ron, and one that has no conclusion. It's apparent that the beings try to make every effort to maintain contact with Ron no matter where he's located.

In 2009, Ron's contact with the alien entities changed slightly, in that he was no longer having visitations from the typical grey type beings, but now communicating with a different type of entity that was brown in color, large round black eyes, an extremely thin body, long arms and long fingers, and with three bumps across the head; one in the middle, one to the right side of the head and another to the left. This entity was very similar to the ones that were seen and captured from a UFO crash in 1996, in Varginha, Brazil.

Another Frightening "Dream"

Early one morning, he abruptly awoke from a "dream" at precisely 1:30 a.m.

In it, he experienced himself lying naked, face down on a table, in a room that appeared to be similar to a laboratory, surrounded by different types of machinery. He noticed a number of alien beings present, all dressed in dull, gray-colored gowns that had hoods on them that covered their faces, but had wide slits where their eyes were located. Their long and boney arms were totally exposed from their gowns. There was another human wearing a white smock present with Ron who told him not to worry about what was going to happen, and that the beings simply wanted to examine him – in particular his head and his back – and that he would not be harmed.

Ron now became fearful, and finding it difficult to control his emotions, began crying and begged the person at the side of him to ask the beings to please leave him alone. A four and a half foot tall entity then walked up to Ron, wearing some kind of a gray uniform. Even though his head was covered, Ron could see that it was quite large. The human began pulling something down from the ceiling that looked like a large waist band, with four long steel hinged rods. He began to attach the device around Ron's waist very tightly, and then proceeded to attach the rods to straps around his arms and legs.

Now hooked up to the machine, Ron noticed how it controlled all of his movements. The entity then began to make a very high-pitched squealing noise, and afterward turned to Ron and said to him telepathically (by his name) not to worry, and that he would be fine. The machine-like device then adjusted Ron to a "spread eagle" position, with his rear lifted up slightly. Telepathically, the entity told Ron that he was now going to get on top of his back, and again not to worry. Ron then suddenly felt his head jerk backwards, where the being then ran its long boney fingers down the front of Ron's face, and inside his mouth. Ron could taste the being's fingers which had a horrible bitter taste to them. He then proceeded to put pressure on the upper part of his mouth, and slowly pulled his fingers out while pushing upwards across Ron's face and stopping at the top of Ron's head. He repeated the action three times.

The being then climbed down from Ron's back and stood to his left side. He turned Ron's head towards him and told him that he had an implant behind his left ear. He then asked the human helping with the process to take Ron in a few moments to where the other humans were located, and then continued to pull very harshly on Ron's left ear. He placed a round metal ball against it, and rubbed his finger across the bump behind the ear. He continued to tell Ron that this was an implant, and that he is to leave it alone and to never remove it. Ron inquisitively asked the being why he needed the implant, but was never answered.

Ron's fear and anxiety had now subsided, after realizing that the being was not going to harm him in anyway. The machine then began to move his body in all directions, spreading his legs apart which Ron felt to be considerably painful, and felt like they were about to snap. Ron shouted out to the being to please stop because of the pain he was experiencing, and in doing so, noticed that the room started to become a fuzzy white. He felt that he was going to pass out. The machine then relaxed Ron's body, and the human unhooked him from the device. Ron was helped off the table, and the being handed him a device, somewhat similar to a "ping-pong" paddle that had three round bumps at the edge, and asked that he hold on to it with his right hand. The being asked him to hold it very tight and under no circumstances to let go of it.

The being then proceeded to walk Ron into a room that was approximately twenty-five by twenty-five feet long, and had many other people sitting in chairs along two walls. The being placed Ron in an empty chair at the end of the row. He noticed that all the people seemed to be in a "switched-off" mode, a trance-like state with their heads bowed down. Ron felt extremely tired after the whole physical examination he had just gone through, almost like he had been sedated and just wanted to sleep. Suddenly, a man sitting by the side of him raised his head and told Ron that he had no idea how lucky he had been. The man didn't give Ron time to answer, and resumed back in his trance-like state. Ron was still holding onto the device.

Three alien beings entered the room, and each one was holding a strange-looking machine. One being held a small box with what looked like a cable and a microphone, and what resembled a back-pack device on his back. The second being had a long flexible tube, and the third had a round object in his hand. They seemed to be just passing through, and within moments another alien being entered with Ron's sister, who was also holding onto an object; an eighteen-inch-long board. She began to tell Ron about it, but Ron couldn't make any sense of what she was saying as she was acting like she was in a trance. Shortly afterward, a being came back to get her and take her out of the room, followed by a human who approached Ron and took him back into the lab. As he did so, the human explained to Ron how lucky he is to be one of the "chosen."

Back in the lab, Ron saw the table that he had just been lying on with the device hanging from the ceiling, and many human people and alien entities working together in the environment. After a while, another being approached Ron and telepathically asked him to follow. He told Ron that his name was Elbi, and that he was going to take Ron somewhere and not to be afraid. Ron was to keep holding on to the paddle-like object in his hand and not to let go of it. As Ron followed Elbi down a long and dark hallway, two "bullet-shaped" droids approached Ron on either side of him. Ron thought to himself how these droids resembled the bullet-shaped trash cans from many years ago, except that these had tubes and lights attached to them. Elbi telepathically told Ron that he had seen way too much for now, and that he would be returning at a later time to show Ron more, and instructed him once again to not let go of the device. Ron felt an unusual connection with this being, a great love for him, so different from the grey entities and past encounters that he had previously experienced.

Suddenly, Ron's surroundings turned hazy, and then he lost consciousness. He awoke to find himself standing on what looked to be a tarmac runway, and still holding onto the device. He noticed that his sister was also present, and still in a trance-like state holding on to the long board. Although it was night time, Ron could see hangers or very large buildings off in the distance. He telepathically heard a voice telling him not to worry, and that "they" were coming to get him. He said goodbye to his sister, and awoke from the alleged dream.

Ron immediately got out of bed and went to the bathroom, looked in the mirror at his left ear which was extremely tender and sore to the touch. He also noticed a red line (scar) on his left shoulder, with a deep purple mark at the top of it. There were two further puncture marks in the center of the red line (which after three days disappeared, but the purple spot remained visible).

The very next day, Ron awoke to find the same mark on the top of his right foot, with three additional purple spots. Throughout the "dream" Ron had no conscious memory of any examinations or procedures, other than to his ear, and felt that it couldn't possibly have been a dream, simply because of the foreign marks on his body. He realized that he had to have been physically present for this experience to have happened.

A few years ago, Ron met Dr. Roger Leir, a pioneer in his field of research, and the main man at the center of performing a number of surgeries to remove alleged alien implants. Ron showed Dr. Leir the implant that was protruding from under the skin behind his left ear, and suggested that he was thinking of having it removed, and that researching the object could perhaps greatly help science in some way. Dr. Leir suggested that he would organize the surgery to remove it, if that's what Ron wanted to do.

Precisely three days later, Ron experienced an alien encounter. He was taken again onboard the craft, and telepathically told that under no circumstances was he to remove the object behind his ear, and that it had to remain where it was, influencing Ron to make the decision to decline from having the surgery after all.

The being named Elbi that Ron had encountered, has continued to make contact with him fairly regularly over the last couple of years until Ron's mother passed away in September 2010. The last contact with Elbi was in May of the same year. During a conversation with him, he telepathically told Ron that his race of beings resided here on earth, but in a different dimension. Ron asked the whereabouts of the location of this other realm on earth, to which Elbi showed a series of symbols that immediately appeared telepathically in Ron's mind. The symbols spelled out the word SISKIYOU, which is a county located in Northern California, adjacent to the Oregon border. He proceeded to tell Ron that they have a base there, and that their ships are present constantly, but in this other dimension.

During one of Ron's encounters with Elbi, a machine-like device was placed in front of Ron. Elbi explained to him what the machine was used for. It was a box-like machine that had a beam of light coming out of the top of it that allowed Elbi and his race to "dimension hop" here on earth, as well as many other places. Ron experienced a downloading of information about the machine directly into his brain, but cannot consciously remember the details. Elbi explained to Ron that he wanted him to try an experiment with the machine. He asked him to place his right foot forward, heel down and with his foot in the air, and that when Ron was ready to dimension hop, to stick his foot out as tightly as he could. Ron followed his instructions and immediately found himself somewhere high up in the mountains within a forest area. He noticed a number of army personnel also present, all wearing camouflage. A soldier approximately 100 feet away from Ron pointed to him and started yelling "there he is, get him," to which Ron became alarmed. As the soldier immediately noticed him, Ron moved his foot backwards and found himself once again in the other dimension with Elbi.

Although shocked at what he had just experienced, Ron was also excited about the very fact that the machine would allow him to travel to another dimension like that, and eager to try it again. Ron took the same steps as before, and found himself exactly in the same place, except that the military were now much closer. They again noticed Ron's presence, and gave orders to grab him. As they began to run forward to Ron, he promptly moved his foot backwards and once again found himself in familiar surroundings with Elbi standing by the machine.

Elbi stated to Ron that our military is very much trying to locate them, and to capture them to find out who their race of beings are, but never will, because they constantly reside in another dimension that is inaccessible to human beings.

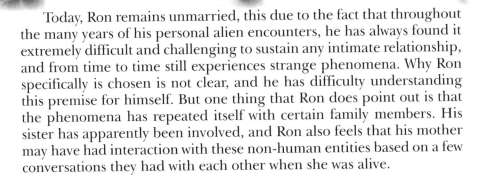

Today, Ron remains unmarried, this due to the fact that throughout the many years of his personal alien encounters, he has always found it extremely difficult and challenging to sustain any intimate relationship, and from time to time still experiences strange phenomena. Why Ron specifically is chosen is not clear, and he has difficulty understanding this premise for himself. But one thing that Ron does point out is that the phenomena has repeated itself with certain family members. His sister has apparently been involved, and Ron also feels that his mother may have had interaction with these non-human entities based on a few conversations they had with each other when she was alive.

Alien Encounters

"When he sees I see him, he comes over to the bed. He looks mean. He's little. Goes up to about the top of the lamp. Looking down at me. Got eyes. Big eyes. Big slanted eyes.... I see pictures of the world just blowing up.... The world turns into a whole red ball of fire. It just seems to burst into flames like a little ball of gasoline out in the middle of the sky.... He took a little thing like a stick – a needle – and when he moved it even so slightly in the air I could see it spark at the end and it went like that (makes striking motion) and it went bang, and spread a tingling all over my face."

~Whitley Strieber

Abduction Experience 1985, New York
Excerpt: his book, *Communion*

Chris's Encounter
Las Vegas, Nevada

Experiencer/Abductee

Ever since Chris was young, she has always had an interest in the unknown – all things supernatural, paranormal, and spiritual. But as Chris got older, she also developed a curiosity for other dimensions, which, of course, involved UFOs. During Chris's life, she has come to experience a number of strange and bizarre encounters that have sometimes involved other worldly beings, so many encounters, in fact, that unfortunately they cannot all be fully presented here due to a lack of conscious recall or not having had hypnotic regression to uncover them. However, the cases that are presented of Chris's conscious memories of her encounters are complete in experience. Chris has also had instances of precognitive dreams that have actually come to light and have been validated on a number of occasions, not to mention her ability to astral travel or remote view various locations and situations at will.

From her earliest memories as a child, she recalls her first paranormal experience of encountering a ghost at the age of ten, only then to later in life experience contact with alien beings. There are various strange happenings that Chris's mother shared with her when Chris got older, as at the time she was too young to remember them. One incident in particular that her mother recalls, is that one moment Chris would be outside playing with her friends, and the next minute she would have totally disappeared! When Chris did eventually return home some hours later, her mother would repeatedly question her as to where she had been, as many hours had passed by. Chris would say that she had been with her friends from another world, which gave her mother the distinct impression that she had been in the company of aliens.

Later, during her school years and at the age of fifteen, Chris and one of her friends began to experience a series of school bullying by a group of girls from a different class. Chris felt that this was because she and her friend were popular and likeable teenagers, and that they were both attractive blonds. On one particular day, the group of girls approached Chris's friend, cornering her and making her feel extremely frightened and anxious as to what their next move would be. But having accomplished their goal of putting her in a place of utter fear, they then turned around and made their way to Chris who was in the school locker room.

As the girls now approached Chris, she decided to put her fear to one side, and standing up to them, turned directly to the bullies, telling them that they ought to seriously think of taking a hike and leaving her alone, because she had friends who were aliens who would not let her be harmed under any circumstance, or by anyone. Within a split second, the girls spun around on their heels, and as quick as their legs could take them, with lightening-like speed bolted from the scene!

When Chris got older and eventually married and had her own family, there would still be occasions when paranormal activity would take place in the home. This time, the incident involved Chris's son, who, at a young age of only four years, would run into Chris's bedroom to tell her that he couldn't sleep because his bed was floating. Although Chris was very interested and curious of the paranormal and other dimensional realities, at the time of the incident, she was too afraid to go and check her son's room to see the floating bed for herself, and so continued to allow him to sleep in her room until he was thirteen years of age! This floating bed incident was so disturbing to him, that he made a point of not wanting to sleep in the bed even with Chris, but instead would sleep on the floor between the bed and the wall where he would feel protected, and would eventually fall asleep.

Some years later, meditation became a passion that Chris developed. A friend of her's approached Chris one time and asked if she would like to attend a meditation group with her, to which Chris agreed. It turned out that she enjoyed the meditation so much, that it became a regular event for her, twice a week for the next five years. In the group, she learned how to use her intuitive abilities and was taught how to channel. But it was at the very first group meeting that Chris recalls a strange incident happening, during the actual meditation itself. Going through the motions of the meditation and with her eyes closed, the process was interrupted by a female calling out Chris's name, telepathically.

Upon hearing her name being called, she immediately opened her eyes and locked on to a strange-looking female sitting some distance in front of her, who happened to be staring back at Chris, and who Chris believed was the one who had called her name. The woman had short red/orange hair, her eyes were quite large and almond shaped, and she had a very small mouth. She was surrounded by what appeared to be male body guards. As soon as the meditation was over, the strange-looking woman and her "body guards" got up from their seats and quickly left.

Chris had an unshakable feeling, a deep knowing that this woman she'd seen in the meditation was a "hybrid" being, or some type of entity in human form, who was not of this earth.

Over the years, there have been a small number of accounts of alien encounters where people have actually seen entities transforming to disguise themselves as human beings. The name given to this has sometimes been referred to as being or transforming into an Avatar. The meaning of *Avatar* originates from ancient Sanskrit, Hindu mythology, and is the manifestation of a deity to the earth in an incarnate form – the manifestation of a being that can appear at will either in human or animal form.

There is a case similar to this involving a well-known remote viewer (psychic spy) named Ingo Swann who tells of an unusual alien encounter in his book *Penetration – The Question of Extraterrestrial and Human Telepathy*. In it, he describes an encounter with an extraterrestrial Avatar in human form as a female, who one day he meets while in a supermarket in California. At the time, Ingo was involved in a super-secret program known as Star Gate.

The book itself is an intriguing read, and discusses undeveloped human telepathy, and explores the fact that the higher echelons or *powers that be*, know more than they're admitting about the moon, it's origins, and even it's occupants.

Later, when Chris reached her thirties, another strange event involving an alien encounter occurred – a conscious memory of being onboard a UFO and having contact with a female alien entity. Although

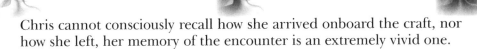
Chris cannot consciously recall how she arrived onboard the craft, nor how she left, her memory of the encounter is an extremely vivid one.

Having arrived on the craft, she found herself sitting in what appeared to be a waiting-room area, where she recalls that, after some time, a female entity made her way to her, and asked her telepathically to follow. Chris described the being to be around six feet tall, very serene, and wearing a robe. Her head was bald, and she had extremely large blue eyes. Her skin was remarkably pale, so pale that Chris likened it to be the color of a very light shade of blue, but made the distinct point that it was definitely not gray.

As Chris followed her, she noticed that the interior of the craft had an ambient lighting to it, a mossy bluish-green color. As she continued to walk around the corner of the ship, she could see the control panels and a wall-to-wall window that was large and curved. Through this window, Chris could see a breathtaking and beautiful sight – the immense vastness of space, dark and endless, with stars upon stars.

The being took Chris from this area into another room, not too far away from the initial waiting room, where there was a large wall that appeared to be made from some type of material similar to a frosted glass or plastic. Behind this wall was dim lighting, and on the wall itself were many little baskets, row upon row. Chris recalls seeing approximately six rows of baskets across the wall, and five rows that ran vertically, a total of thirty in all. She had the distinct impression that this room was some type of a nursery, or even an incubatorium.

The female walked over to one of the baskets and handed Chris a very tiny baby from it, and placed it in her arms. Immediately, Chris thought how cute the tiny baby was with its extremely large blue eyes, and watched in amazement as it wrapped its tiny hand around one of Chris's fingers. She had the feeling that the female entity wanted her to interact with the baby, as she watched Chris intently to see her emotional reaction to it. Chris knew that there was a baby in every single basket, but the female only handed one particular baby to her. Onboard the craft, Chris remembers only having contact with the female and the baby, and saw no other beings at that time. Her encounter is a conscious one, and up to this point, she has not pursued hypnotic regression.

In June 1994, a camping trip revealed yet another strange experience for Chris. A trip to Cold Creek Canyon in Las Vegas, where Chris and her friend, Paula, decided to go on a retreat at the camping grounds so that Paula could teach her about Indian medicine and the various methods of Indian cooking, as Paula was of Lakota Indian decent.

Half way through the evening, Chris had an uncomfortable feeling that something was not quite right, and told Paula that they should immediately get into their vehicle. Both afraid, they jumped in the car, leaving all of their camping equipment and food in the area where they had been sitting. Forty minutes passed by, and nothing happened. So they began to relax and chat for awhile, rolling down the windows and dangling their feet outside. At precisely 3 a.m., they noticed an emerald green object streak across the sky traveling from the East. They watched as it suddenly exploded, appearing to catch fire before seemingly land somewhere in the West.

They both jumped out of the car, and stood close by the vehicle still looking up at the sky. Immediately, another object came over head, this time a gray cigar-shaped UFO. They observed the object for what they thought to be five minutes, where Chris started to shout at the craft "We're here, we're here, come and get us." Paula was completely afraid of it and asked Chris to please stop shouting at it, because she felt a negative *vibe* from it. (It's interesting to note that in some UFO cases, experiencers/abductees have repeatedly talked about cigar-shaped UFOs having reptilian occupants in them. These beings are not considered friendly by any means, and in the majority of cases reported, experiencers have not had positive interactions with them.)

Suddenly, Chris felt once again that something was terribly wrong. She quickly turned to look at her vehicle and saw what she thought to be a Coyote climbing into it. Chris became terrified of it, and managed to physically lift Paula (a fairly heavy-set woman) and place her in front of Chris and the car door, shouting repeatedly to her to get the animal out! Chris noticed the animal moving in a very unusual fashion for that of a coyote (if indeed it was a coyote) and watched it *slither* out of the car. Both ladies, now frantic because of what they had just seen, jumped back into the car and drove off in the dark, not knowing where they were heading. They eventually reached another camp ground where they decided to stay for the night, even though they had left their sleeping bags back at the other camp ground, and were too terrified to go back after the experience they'd had.

The following morning, a ranger came over to the campsite and asked everyone to leave the area. Chris decided to share the details with him of the experience with the "animal" the night before. Once hearing their story, the ranger walked up to Chris's vehicle and looked inside it. He noticed very large paw prints on the dash board, and said that it was actually a mountain lion that had climbed into Chris's car. This, he said, was probably due to something starting a fire up in the mountains to the West, that had pushed the animals to seek safety on lower ground. Another interesting observation made by the ranger was that he had only seen the paw prints around Chris's vehicle and nowhere else on the campsite!

When Chris and Paula arrived back at their original campsite, they noticed the tire marks from where their vehicle had been parked the previous night, and saw the animals paw prints from where it had circled the car. The odd thing about it was that there was a second set of foot prints by the side of the larger ones that had three toes at the front and one toe at the back, similar to a chicken, but it was as if the animal or creature had been walking forward with it's back toe at the front! Observing these prints, Paula told Chris that the lion had in fact been a "shape shifter," and as a Lakota Indian, she knew of such stories of beings shape-shifting into animal forms, and linked the experience to the cigar-shaped UFO they had seen overhead.

On leaving the site at the ranger's request, Chris had lost all sense of direction as to which road to take to exit the grounds, and as they followed a dirt road that led them up and over a hill, they were shocked to see a metallic object embedded in the ground and many military men surrounding it. Chris was convinced that the object was a UFO; it was somewhat disc-shaped with half of it embedded fairly deep into the dirt. It was completely roped off, and within minutes, a black helicopter flew over head, shortly followed by fireman who were all dressed in black uniforms, who also surrounded the object. She noticed dark blue trucks that definitely belonged to the Air Force but were disguised as "Gardening" and "Plumbing" trucks, obviously to distract attention from what was going on.

Chris bravely ventured towards the men to ask them what was happening, while Paula stayed in the vehicle. As soon as she approached them, the men, without any hesitation, immediately turned towards Chris and, without further ado, escorted her back to the vehicle where Paula was waiting and asked them to leave. As Chris began driving out of the area and heading towards home, she and Paula had a lengthy discussion about the strange weekend camping trip, the crashed disc, and the men who were guarding it. Paula shared her thoughts about the object and that she too felt it was a spaceship that had crashed on the hillside, and that it was responsible for creating the fire that had caused the wildlife to move down towards the campsite. The incident was, without a doubt, hushed up, as Chris and Paula never heard any further news reported about it.

In 1995, Chris had yet another encounter with extraterrestrials. This is a conscious memory which required no hypnotic regression, and although this incident is a relatively short one, it is a bizarre one, as it involved a joint encounter with a friend of Chris's who had also continuously experienced alien encounters throughout her life.

One morning, during the early hours at approximately 3 a.m., Chris was suddenly jolted awake for what seemed to be no apparent reason. As soon as she awoke, she saw a "door" appear over her bed. Chris felt that the intense jolting movement was, in fact, due to having been "dropped" from a fair height above her bed. Within a second or two of the experience, the telephone rang. Her friend was calling to tell Chris of a strange experience that she had just had, being with Chris somewhere completely strange, and immediately woke up after the feeling of being "dropped" from a height onto her bed.

It appears that in their joint encounter, they found themselves in a room where the atmosphere was extremely smoky, a place that was dark with gray tones and many male entities. The strange thing about these entities was that they all appeared to have no faces. This gave Chris and her friend the impression that they somehow were not allowed to reveal their facial features. Chris's friend, having had so many alien encounters of her own, had a deep knowing that these beings were all reptilian, as she had experienced these same type of entities and their negative vibration on other occasions during previous encounters. (Quite often, in cases where experiencers have witnessed seeing reptilian beings, they have reported that sometimes these entities haven't shown their physical features so as not to alarm the experiencer of their true reptilian form.)

Although Chris was extremely curious of her surroundings, and wanted to explore the environment further, her friend did not want to stay a moment longer, and continued to try and pull Chris away from the situation. Her friend succeeded, and the encounter ended at this point where both women found themselves back in their beds only to be suddenly awakened by a "dropping" sensation, which Chris attributed to be from falling from the mysterious door over her bed!

In the mid '90s, Chris attended an astral travel lecture given by George Knapp, a very well-known Investigative Journalist for a local Television Channel in Las Vegas. After the lecture, Chris became extremely interested and anxious to try it for herself. She was a member of an "energy" group in Las Vegas that experimented with various forms of energy through meditation, and a friend of hers who lived in Canada at the time also ran an energy group that focused on the same subject. Both groups decided that on a certain day and time, they would experiment with astral travel, and Chris decided that her focus and mission of astral traveling was going to be at the location of Area 51.

Once in a meditative state and experiencing being in the zone of astral traveling, Chris found herself driving in a jeep that was losing control as she drove through a ravine, and within moments the vehicle ended up turning on its side throwing Chris out of it. Immediately, she felt the need to hide, as coming up a long stretch of road was an army of very small men in many, many jeeps, heading away from what appeared to be the super-secret base of Area 51. At a distance, she thought the men to be "Peruvians" as they were fairly dark skinned and what she thought to be Indian looking, but as they came much closer Chris realized that they were, in fact, all grey beings.

Chris now extremely fearful of what was heading her way, knew that these beings were trying to keep her out of the area. There was no place that she could escape to take her out of this terrifying situation. Suddenly, a 7- to 8-foot-tall humanoid entity appeared in front of her, a Nordic-type being with short blond hair and extremely beautiful blue eyes that were almond-shaped and emitted a whitish, sparkling crystalline energy from them. He was exceptionally handsome. He was *so* handsome that he reminded Chris of a Michael Angelo statue, as his features were perfectly angular – she became enamored by his beautiful appearance.

Chris knew that he was there to rescue her from the small grey beings, and the next thing she remembered, she was of being taken into some kind of a cave. She noticed that this cave was made of black granite that had etchings on its walls. Not able to make out what the inscriptions and writings were, the Nordic being lifted Chris up high on his shoulders and told her telepathically to place her hands on the wall so that she could

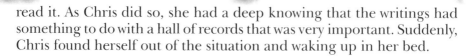
read it. As Chris did so, she had a deep knowing that the writings had something to do with a hall of records that was very important. Suddenly, Chris found herself out of the situation and waking up in her bed.

Later that morning, Chris received a phone call from her friend in Canada who facilitated the energy group, along with a second call from a friend in Las Vegas. All three ladies had a three-way conversation about Chris's experience during her astral travel. Chris decided that it was important to draw what she had actually witnessed at the base – the terrain, the runways, the front of the buildings that appeared to go underground, etc., just in case someone, somewhere, might be able to later verify her description of Area 51 itself.

Some time after this astral travel session, Chris decided to experiment with the process again, and found herself at an Air Force base, wandering around and observing what was going on. A few months later, while visiting a friend of hers in Georgia, who happened to be a Colonel, he took her for a visit to a remote base that was located in the middle of a forest area. He proceeded to interrogate her with numerous questions, and asked what she had been doing out at MacDill Air Force base recently, as she had been seen there by some of the military men.

Chris then realized that the astral travel experiment had obviously worked, and that she had developed a talent for it. But she denied to the Colonel the fact she'd ever been at the base and repeatedly argued the case that the men must have mistaken her identity for someone else. He proceeded to argue back and forth that the description the men gave fit her completely. Chris stayed silent about the astral travel experiment, and continued to deny ever having a presence there.

Chris is an exceptionally talented lady. Not only have her experiences been with extraterrestrials, but she has also interacted with, and has a deep passion for, meditation and astral travel. Today, Chris's extraterrestrial encounters have somewhat subsided, although she does not have any idea why this is the case. She has expressed a certain amount of sadness because of this, and would love for her encounters to manifest once again.

Alien Encounters

"The beings were small. Were three- to five-feet tall, had very large, pear shaped heads, with gray skin, large dark almond-shaped eyes, tiny holes for noses, and ears, slit-like mouth, and a very little neck. They had a body, legs with boots, arms, and hands with only three fingers. They wore a blue tight fitting suit, with a belt and body strap across their chest. An eagle insignia was on their upper arm. They gave off a feeling of peace, communicated through mental telepathy, and levitated in a smooth fashion as they moved. My father was the only one that saw them in a hopping-type walk. However, we did not walk up the stairs when we entered the craft. We hopped past the stairs as we went inside."

~Betty Andreasson Luca

Abduction Experience 1967, Massachusetts
Excerpt: BJ's Interview with Abductee Betty
Andreasson Luca
UFO Casebook: The Abduction of Betty Andreasson Luca

Alien Beings

Artwork by Kesara

Grey Alien Being. This type of being is the most common and predominant amongst the alien beings observed – usually gray in color, approximately four-feet tall in height, and associated with the metallic disc-shaped craft.

Reptilian Being. This type of being is very often known to have a negative or aggressive type of disposition, and on the occasion, has been seen onboard craft alongside the grey entities. They are usually associated with the cigar-shaped UFO sightings.

Nordic Being. Nordic beings are known to resemble the human being, except that their features are perfectly angular. They are benevolent and positive beings, oftentimes associated with performing healing onboard the craft.

Dwarf Alien Being. The Dwarf being is often referred to as a trickster, one who likes to play games with the experiencer, and has often been seen pulling the bed covers off the individual, or tickling the experiencer as they lie sleeping.

Tall White Being. These beings are noted as being the tallest; the mature being is often seen to be 8.5 feet tall. They are not seen as frequently as the other entities, in particular the "greys," and are apparently only connected to the Indian Springs location.

Alien Implants in Humans Fact or Fiction ???

By Dr. Roger K. Leir, DPM

If someone had told me thirty years ago that I would become the world's leading researcher on the subject of Alien Implants in human beings, I would have thought they were totally insane. My science background, training, and work grounded me in a severe state of scientific skepticism. It was not hard for me to believe we were not the only so-called intelligent living entities in this vast, little-understood universe, and to also believe in the possibility these intelligences have been visiting this planet for thousands, or even millions, of years. But to consider the invasive aspect of abductions and its related mysteries of implantation in humans with unknown foreign objects was just too much for me to swallow.

My first endeavor into the removal of these objects was the result of an effort to prove one UFO researcher a thorough nut case. This was in 1995. Two surgeries were performed for the removal of metallic objects that were verified on an x-ray prior to surgery and to me represented nothing more than ordinary metallic foreign bodies, which I'd had surgically extracted many times previously. Since my profession is a foot surgeon, and having practiced over 47 years, I feel that I am somewhat of an expert on foreign bodies which individuals get instilled into their bodies on a daily basis. Nothing was to prepare me for the surprises I had in store: It was as if opening the proverbial Pandora's Box.

To date, our surgical team from our 501(c)(3) nonprofit research organization has performed sixteen surgeries and submitted them for extensive biological and metallurgical analysis by some of the worlds most famous laboratories such as Los Alamos National Labs, New Mexico Tech, York University, University of Toronto, and Seal Labs in Southern California, just to mention a few.

Our findings have been astonishing and include the following:

- No inflammatory or rejection reaction by the body

- Ingrowths of specialized nerve cells

- No visible scar or portal of entry

- Emissions of electromagnetic fields when in the body prior to removal

- Radio signal emissions

- Metallurgical findings which include: meteoric iron; rare earth elements; non-terrestrial isotopic ratios; carbon nano-structures; selective isotopes, which can not exist alone in nature; strange shaped objects, such as ovoids, spheres, and rectangular crystals of varying sizes

We have recently been able to calculate that the materials composing the last two surgically extracted objects come from one third the way across the Milky Way Galaxy and represent a civilization at least 30 million years older than we are.

I have presented my findings in forty-two countries and have authored seven books on this subject. (Alienscalpel.com)

~**Dr. Roger K. Leir, DPM**

Alien Encounters

"One night, an eerie green glow lit up the formation; and on another evening, strange "white glowing humanoid figures" were seen moving about in the forest depths by campers. One young couple asleep in their tent on another night, were woken up by a bright, silvery glow that enveloped their two-man tent. Thinking it to be torches of other campers that might have made their way along the Ruined Castle track in the dark, the couple emerged to see a 1.8m [nearly 5 feet 11 inches]tall, "human-like glowing form," as they said later. It immediately strode up to the woman, appeared to grasp her with both its arms, then pass right through her. At this point she fainted, while before her shocked male companion, the "human-light form" appeared to fade away to nothing."

~Rex and Heather Gilroy

Excerpt: *Blue Mountains Triangle*
Chapter Thirteen – "Abductions by the Energy
Beings"

Interview with
Dr. Roger K. Leir, DPM

Several years ago, I had the pleasure of interviewing my dear, and longtime friend, Dr. Roger Leir, on a paranormal television show that I produced and hosted entitled: *Let's Talk Paranormal*. He was an extremely gracious guest, and spoke in depth about this strange, yet fascinating, subject of alien encounters/abductions that have resulted with the implantation of small objects in various areas of abductees' bodies.

During the interview, Dr. Leir spoke of the first two surgeries that were performed on August 19, 1995. The individuals who had these strange objects in their bodies were supported by x-ray evidence, and the objects themselves were found to be "alien implants." One of the experiencers, a female, had two objects in her great toe. The second case, a male, had an object in the back of his hand. Dr. Leir explained to me that his decision to perform these surgeries was, in fact, to disprove the whole alien implant theory, and that he'd thought it to be nothing more than sheer nonsense.

The two cases were initially referred to him by a researcher who was heavily involved with the alien abduction field, and showed Dr. Leir the x-rays, explaining in great length as to why he and the abductees believed the objects to be of alien origin. Dr. Leir decided to challenge the researcher by suggesting that he have the implants removed from the two individuals, and that he would then further investigate what the objects actually were.

The researcher added that the experiencers were willing to have the objects removed, but unfortunately had no funds to pay for the surgeries, as well as having no medical insurance that would help to cover some of the cost. Dr. Leir proposed that if the individuals could make their way to California, he would be willing to perform the surgeries with no charge.

He asked for the x-ray showing the implant in the back of the gentleman's hand to be sent to his radiologist so that he could take a look at it. He then proceeded to ask a surgeon, a friend of his, if he would be willing to perform the surgery, to which he agreed, and both surgeries were completed on the same day.

Dr. Leir has been a practicing podiatrist for some forty years, and during that time, had surgically removed many things from the human body. Coral, paper, hair, glass – you name it and he's taken it out of the foot. But he adds that when you enter into the body and there's no scarification to begin with, you remove a "T" -shaped object, and then, looking at it closely, see that it's wrapped in a strange type of clinging "glove-like" membrane that's gray in color, and then take a surgical blade to try to cut through it and find it can't be cut, this is indeed something very different from normal, everyday items that are usually removed.

Dr. Leir then began to remove another object from the opposite side of the patients toe, which was similar in shape to that of a small "cantaloupe seed," again covered in a strange membrane. He and his team tried to cut through it, and once more met with great disappointment.

The second surgery was to remove the object from the back of the gentleman's hand, which turned out to be exactly the same as the small cantaloupe seed object that was previously removed from the lady's toe. This in itself was mind-boggling to Dr. Leir and his team, and once again this object was shown to be covered in the same strange, gray type, well-organized membrane that couldn't be cut with a surgical blade.

As time passed, and more surgeries of implant removal were performed, Dr. Leir noticed that there was a common thread to *all* of them. There was *no portal of entry* to how these objects had found their way into the body. Nothing seemed out of place. He used magnification to look for any type of scarring, no matter how minute, but found nothing. His thoughts were that if these beings had a technology that was so far advanced to get them here from someone else, or *through* somewhere else, that by having this kind of technology, then maybe they had the ability to enter into a living body and place something inside it, or take something *out* without physically interrupting the molecular structure of the skin, or the tissue. Dr. Leir also raised the point that scientists are not certain if these beings are extraterrestrial, inter-dimensional, time travelers, or all of the above. The patients are just as intrigued and baffled at the strange objects removed from their bodies.

Part of the criteria and protocols for the removal of the implants is that Dr. Leir's non-profit organization, *A & S Research*, which has been created to undertake scientific studies of these objects, becomes the owner of the implants. The individual agrees to sign consent to this, and once the funding is in place, the objects are then sent to the laboratories where they are analyzed for biological and metallurgical aspects. The objects are sub-divided into various groups. One group is labeled "non metallic" with a biological coating. The second group is labeled "non metallic," and the third group is labeled "biological."

To be considered for the removal of an object, Dr. Leir expresses that the individual firstly has to have had some exposure to the UFO phenomenon. Secondly, they should not have undergone regression hypnosis prior to the surgery, so that whatever the experiencer has experienced with a conscious memory has served adequate time into the area of research, and brings forth how the individual feels about it.

Each experiencer is also examined by a psychological team both prior to and after the surgery. Many of the experiencers have made the interesting comment that after the removal of the objects, they felt a "new-found feeling of freedom," which in itself is a very intriguing comment.

It's interesting to note that *all* of the strange objects removed to date have been found by scientific laboratories to be of extreme interest, and at the time of this book going to print, Dr. Leir has removed sixteen alleged alien implants.

After years of being asked what the actual purpose of these objects could be, Dr. Leir has come to the conclusion that they are for genetic monitoring purposes, and personally believes that for thousands of years, the human race has been, and still is, being genetically manipulated. He performed a specific study of seventeen functional growth characteristics in children, and compared them over a forty-year period from 1947 to 1987. He found that there was a sixteen to eighty percent accelerated change, which is a very high number for such a short period of time. Why is this happening?

He posed the possibility of it being connected to evolution, but thought this not to be the case. The next area for consideration was the environment and all of the environmental factors – the depletion of the ozone layer, the bombardment of cosmic rays, and other high-energy particles. Could this also be a contributing factor? Pollution of the atmosphere perhaps? He added that if we look at these scenarios on a geographical level, we find that these changes are worldwide, and so we have a myriad of different changes that are taking place in the environment, and yet these statistics remain the same. Therefore, if a child survives, then these statistics become true. He stated that if we rule out the environment and evolution, this then only leads to two other possibilities: Either it's an act of God, or if we are not satisfied with that answer and have more of an inquisitive and open mind, the only other possibility is that the human race is being genetically manipulated. This takes us back to the question: Why have an implant in the human body?

There have been other theories put forth, such as devices to track the individual, which was demonstrated in Steven Spielberg's television series *Taken*. Are they devices for measuring the changes of chemicals or pollution in our bodies? Dr. Leir does not believe that it's either one of these scenarios, but that it has to do with monitoring genetics.

I had asked Dr. Leir whether any particular country supports this extraordinary subject and the finding of alleged alien implants. He stated that, by traveling all over the world, as he has done so many times, to lecture at various UFO conferences, he has found that his participating audiences are fascinated with the implant cases that he puts forth. After the event, many members of the audience have approached him to talk about their own personal experiences. This is how Dr. Leir finds more and more individual cases and acknowledges that this phenomena is really world-wide. Not only are these cases involved with the alien encounter/abduction phenomena itself, but there are other aspects to the phenomena that are also involved, such as sightings of strange craft, and individuals who report to have these strange objects in their body, many times having had either an x-ray, a CAT scan, or an MRI to prove it.

In some instances, there are experiencers who have had an object in a certain area of their bodies, but did not want to have it removed. Dr. Leir does not try to persuade the individual to remove it, unless of course the object itself is causing them some kind of distress, either physiological or psychological, and only then he expresses that perhaps they should think about having it removed.

There was a case in Brazil that Dr. leir had been working with some time ago, where a woman had two objects placed in her left great toe, and did not want to have them removed. She had specifically been told by whoever had placed them there that she should not remove them, and so was very fearful about having them taken out. They showed her a demonstration that was most likely to intimidate her, of being able to stop an insect in mid-air with some kind of a beam of light, and told her that no matter where this particular insect traveled on the planet, they could find this specific insect anywhere.

Dr. Leir adds that if we stop and think about this scenario for a moment, and compare it to knowledge we have today, we know for example that DNA has an electronic signature, and we all have different DNA, and so if alien beings have a device or apparatus that is sensitive enough to look at specific DNA signatures, we can do exactly the same thing – so it's not that fantastic. But the other aspect that it proves is that these objects are *not* tracking devices, and that a civilization that is so far advanced does not require a device to track a living thing on this planet.

The question is then, if the objects are for genetic purposes, are these beings selecting people with specific blood types, and could this be the reason why all of humanity doesn't become implanted with one?

Dr. Leir thought this to be a very good question, and stated that there's been a little work done on blood typing of various individuals. He stated that it is a fact that the abductions occur within families, and that they are indeed following family lineage, and so upon being taken by these beings and having interaction with them, it's highly likely that the experiencers *mother* and *grandmother* have been taken also, and so following the family lineage is extremely important to them.

How do we move forward then with this knowledge, and with the evidence of alien implants? To conclude, Dr. Leir feels that this knowledge should not be kept secret, nor should it be stored away some place in a secret cabal, government, or organization. He believes that our planet is indeed being visited by Extraterrestrials, and most probably has been for thousands of years. This knowledge, he states, should be made available to the public worldwide, because the knowledge does indeed belong to the people of this planet!

Alien Encounters

"I found myself standing in that abandoned carnival yard, clear-headed and fully conscious. There were these creatures again, and I could see that holograms of human faces were cast over their faces, to disguise their true appearance and make me feel less apprehensive. I noticed that each alien seemed to be concentrating and communicating or transmitting its thoughts to the creature to my left. They seemed to be of like mind, as though combining their consciousness into one telepathic voice."

~Jim Sparks

Abduction Experience 1988, Florida
Excerpt: *The Keepers: An Alien Message for the Human Race*

John's Encounter
Southern California

Experiencer/Abductee

John began having extraterrestrial experiences at an early age of around four or five years old, where he would sometimes see nonhuman grey entities appear in his bedroom at night, and would often experience physically being taken onboard their craft and as frequently as two or three times a month. Although at the time, being so young, John wasn't fully aware of the reality of actually being onboard a space ship as such until much later. But he knew that he was somewhere else, somewhere other than his own familiar surroundings, and was in the presence of "strange looking doctors" as he would call them.

John's first memory of an encounter was when he was approximately four and half years old. He awoke one morning to hear noises outside the house, and went to the bedroom window to look out. It was around 4:30 a.m. as the sky was beginning to get lighter and dawn was slowly starting to break. John saw a UFO over the house, emitting a yellow light which covered the entire rooftop. At that point, he blacked out. He awoke at 8 a.m. that morning with heavy blood stains down the front of his body, and with memories of being held down by someone and having something forcefully shoved high up inside his nose that reached up into his head. That morning, John's mother questioned him as to what had happened during the night, to which John replied that he didn't know. His mother simply suspected that it was nothing more than a heavy nose bleed.

As John grew older, conscious memories and recollections of bizarre encounters continued, and would sometimes surface in the form of strange dreams. Although John would eventually share his experiences with his parents, who then became aware of his childhood encounters, they would never tell him that it was just a dream or that it was just his imagination playing tricks. This made John believe that they actually knew much more about these beings than they cared to talk about.

Years later, John's mother openly discussed with him that, while pregnant with John, she was carrying twins, but within four to five months of the pregnancy, one of the twins suddenly disappeared in-utero. The doctor had acknowledged that his mother was indeed pregnant with twins and could hear two separate heartbeats, but much later into the term of the pregnancy, one of the heartbeats was no longer present, and only one fetus existed.

John believed that in light of his own personal encounters, that his mother must have also experienced various encounters with these beings in her life. He was of the opinion that an abduction by these grey entities had taken place while she was pregnant, and that his twin was obviously taken by them. It's widely reported within the UFO community that these beings do have a fascination and interest in identical twins. Over the years, there have been various cases that have surfaced where a twin was removed while in utero during an abduction, and cases where both twins have been observed and had interaction with these entities from a young age, only then to be continued throughout their lives.

When John eventually married and had a family of his own, the encounters still continued – not only for John, but also for his wife and children. His wife in particular has had a very difficult time dealing with her personal encounters, especially in light of her upbringing, being a very religious one. Within those religious teachings by her parents, she was told that humanity is all that there is and that life doesn't exist elsewhere; but if it does, then it is likely to be the work of the devil himself. But in spite of conforming to that particular belief system, she has come to the realization that this earthly environment is definitely not all that there is, and has awakened to the fact that it is *she* who has to deal with the fact that these nonhuman grey entities appear in *her* room at night, and not her parents.

In 1999, one very interesting incident occurred when John and his wife were vacationing in Flagstaff, Arizona. Upon arriving at the hotel, they decided that the next day they would make an early start to take a trip to the Grand Canyon. It was while at the Grand Canyon the next night, at around 9 p.m., that John's wife suddenly had a burning desire to visit Sedona. He thought it was a strange idea that she should want to visit the area so late at night and didn't have a good feeling about it, but his wife was adamant and John couldn't talk her out of it.

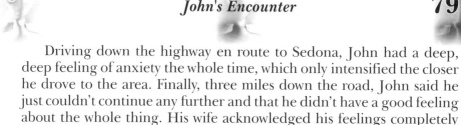

Driving down the highway en route to Sedona, John had a deep, deep feeling of anxiety the whole time, which only intensified the closer he drove to the area. Finally, three miles down the road, John said he just couldn't continue any further and that he didn't have a good feeling about the whole thing. His wife acknowledged his feelings completely and agreed that they should turn around and drive back to the hotel. When they did arrive back, they noticed that the trip had taken a lot longer than it should have, and yet Sedona was not that far away.

That night, and subsequent nights that followed, his wife began having a series of strange dreams in which she felt that she was being closely watched by *someone*, which eventually led to a breakthrough in her consciously remembering that they had indeed been abducted. This encounter had taken place in the middle of the road just before they turned around to head back to the hotel.

Over the next day or so, as John's wife continued to remember and talk about the encounter, it also triggered John's conscious memory, and brought forth fragments of the nightly incident. What actually transpired was that as they turned round a slight bend in the road, a large UFO approximately 100 feet in diameter sat hovering above a clearing, clearly waiting for them to arrive. He thought how *they* must have been monitoring him and his wife telepathically as they drove along the highway, tuning into their thoughts and intentions.

Upon seeing the UFO and immediately becoming afraid, his wife shouted for John to hurry and step on the gas. John quickly tried to turn the car around, but the UFO suddenly aimed a beam of light directly at the car. The beings telepathically told John to stop the vehicle and to wait. His wife was then shockingly pulled upwards through the seat belt, and up through the roof of the car and into the waiting craft.

Ten to fifteen minutes had passed by and John was becoming worried and greatly concerned for his wife's safety. He sat and waited as they had requested him to do, and after a while, they did return her back to the vehicle the same way they had taken her. At that point, both of their conscious memories of what had transpired were totally switched off. They remembered nothing. It is at this precise point of their anxiety getting the better of them, that they decided to turn the car around and head back to the hotel.

It's interesting to note that John's wife was one week pregnant with their older son when this encounter occurred, and in John's subsequent abductions, they had communicated to him that, while onboard, they had given his wife an exam where they had injected her abdomen, similar to our own medical procedure of amniocentesis, which he believes was for the purpose of genetic modification to their son to enhance his capabilities.

He asked the beings to refrain from interacting with his wife, to please leave her alone, and to stop performing these types of examinations on her. They replied that they would as long as she didn't become pregnant again. It is in John's opinion that his children are very important to them.

According to John and many other abductees, genetic modification seems to be very much a part of the beings' own breeding program where alien-human hybrids are concerned. They tend to choose humans who are already genetically interesting to them, and build on those characteristics of interest.

Their children have also had experiences of interaction with these nonhuman entities. They sometimes hear a low humming sound of the craft, similar to that of an aboriginal horn and often a telepathic-type communication. At other times, the sound is heard physically from outside the house – yet no craft is visible at the time. John's three-year-old daughter told him one night how she was scared of the garbage truck that came to pick up the weekly trash, because seeing it, the size of it reminded her of the strange spaceship and of the little grey beings who would take her up into the sky at night!

John periodically examines the children's bodies with an inflorescent light that detects certain stains on them, as there are three common residues sometimes left behind by the beings' finger prints after they have made physical contact with the children. These three colors can range from a yellowish-green to an orange or blue tone in color. John and his wife do not ask the children questions as to what they specifically experience or see, as they are so very young and do not want to traumatize them in anyway. Instead, they wait for the children to openly tell *them* of their experiences.

It's not uncommon for experiencers to see other abductees onboard the craft, and this has been the case for John. On one occasion, a friend openly discussed how he had seen both John and one of his sons together onboard the craft during one particular abduction!

One of the most significant encounters that John recalls is the night that he was taken by the entities and then implanted with an object in his second largest toe of the left foot. He has a clear and conscious memory of this, and of being onboard their ship, and watched as they inserted the strange-looking object. The following morning, after the encounter, John awoke with pain in the toe where the object had been implanted. He noticed there were a few small blood spots on the bed sheet, as well as a couple of red marks on the toe itself.

That day, John began to search for a podiatrist on the Internet to have his toe checked, as the pain increased considerably when he stood and put any type of pressure on it. He found Dr. Roger Leir practically on his doorstep, and made an appointment to meet with him. At Dr. Leir's office, John completed the necessary paperwork as a new patient, and did not divulge any information about the strange object, but only that he was experiencing pain.

After Dr. Leir had examined him, he suggested that John have an x-ray to see what might be causing the pain, just in case there happened to be an injury to a joint. The following week, John met with Dr. Leir again to look at the x-rays. Dr. Leir had looked at them before John arrived to his office, and asked John if he remembered stepping on anything, to which he replied *no*. As Dr. Leir handed John the x-ray, he pointed out the foreign object in the toe, and that it was metallic!

John then openly told Dr. Leir that he knew he had the object in there, and that he is *one of those people* who have that kind of experience. Dr. Leir asked what kind of experience that was, and John replied *alien abduction*. He continued to tell Dr. Leir that he consciously remembered seeing grey entities in the bedroom that night while his wife lay sleeping – who was apparently "switched off" before they appeared and took John onboard the craft. On the craft, John was able to see the apparatus that the alien beings used to insert the implant.

Dr. Leir explained to John that if he wished to pursue this further, he could provide him with a questionnaire that asked a series of questions about his alien encounter experience. The doctor inquired whether John wanted to have the object removed, and John replied that he did.

John completed the questionnaire along with a series of drawings, and the surgery to remove the metallic object was scheduled.

John's Implant Removal Surgery

John had the object removed in 2008. It turned out to be yet another of the "metallic rod" type implants that Dr. Leir had seen in a few other previous cases. It was approximately ¼ inch (6-7mm) in length, and the diameter of a lead pencil.

During the surgery and while trying to remove the object, it unexpectedly began to break into tiny fragments. Dr. Leir and his team had to literally take out the object piece-by-piece. While doing so, a very strange incident occurred. Dr. Leir placed the other fragments into a small vile containing John's blood serum to protect the specimen, leaving only one piece of the object in John's toe. As he went back to remove the last fragment, to everyone's astonishment, the remaining piece totally disappeared!

Everyone present in the operating room witnessed the final piece of the object being there; no-one had removed it or had done anything to it. It just literally disappeared. They had no idea what had happened to it. Dr. Leir's opinion was that either it was under some form of external control that made it invisible, or that the beings themselves had taken it back remotely.

The container which had the small pieces of the implant was then refrigerated for approximately twenty-four to forty-eight hours. When Dr. Leir checked on the specimen to see if everything was okay, to his amazement, all of the tiny, light gray fragments had turned a dark gray in color, and interestingly enough, had began to reassemble themselves in the order in which they were in the body! *How could they reassemble themselves without some kind of a magnetic memory that would need to be present?* Dr. Leir thought.

While placing these small gray fragments under an electron microscope, Dr. Leir and his team saw that they contained structures they hadn't seen before, as well as carbon nano-structures, which are similar to that of electronic machines, and can emit an electromagnetic field, which Dr. Leir and his team had found before the object was ever removed from the body. It emitted a very dense electromagnetic field of between six to eight MGAUSS, which is twice the electromagnetic field of a professional television camera. They came to the conclusion that the object served as a magnetic, electronic device, which also emitted radio frequencies on the FM band width, 1 KHZ range and 1 MHZ range.

Prior to the surgery, another strange incident transpired as John was traveling from his home to undergo an "interview shoot" at Dr. Leir's office. On his way to the office, he drove a distance through an isolated canyon and seemed to have had some missing time, as he didn't arrive for the interview until much later than expected. The television crew and Dr. Leir waited patiently for John to arrive, who later called the office to say that his car had unexpectedly stalled in the middle of the canyon, and that he literally had to walk to the bottom of it to locate someone to tow the car.

At that point, Dr. Leir and few of the crew members jumped into a van and headed to John's location, arriving just before the tow truck. As the driver from the tow truck peered inside to look at the engine, it was apparent to him that one of the electronic components was totally "fried." John's car was not an old vehicle, but a well-kept Cadillac in excellent condition, and everyone was puzzled as to why an electronic component should suddenly be destroyed.

Arriving back at the office, John was taken to the building next door to Dr. Leir's office so that he could undergo a CAT scan that would be used for the television interview segment. The crew asked to see John's x-rays also. They were on 11" x 9" film situated in an x-ray folder clearly labeled: "X-Rays Do Not Bend!" This envelope was laying on Dr. Leir's office desk situated in the middle of the pile of envelopes.

Dr. Leir took John's folder from the middle of the pile to the facility were the radiologist was located. As they took the x-rays out from the envelope and put them up to view on the computer, all of the writing that had been printed on the outside of the envelope was now transferred onto the film itself which had already been developed! This was the only envelope sitting in the middle of the pile that had the writing from the envelope transferred to each one of the films!

Both he and the radiologist were dumbfounded at what they were seeing. Leir asked the radiologist how something like this could possibly happen. The radiologist replied that he had no idea and that this was the first time he had *ever* seen something like this. The radiologist took the x-rays to one of his technicians to ask if he had an explanation that might shed light on what had just happened. The technician took a good long look at the x-rays, scratched his head, and replied that it was impossible!

In Dr. Leir's opinion, there was definitely some kind of an intervention by the alien entities that day, who displayed a wonderful sense of humor throughout the whole undertaking of the implant removal.

John's Recent Experiences

In light of John's encounters with the beings, over time, he has become much more accustomed to them. His encounters can take place as often as twice a week to twice a month, but can also be absent for two months at a time.

While onboard the craft, John is usually met by a being or two, who accompanies him into a room to communicate with him, either on a screen or telepathically, various catastrophic and devastating events to the earth that will take place in the near future. They have, however, not divulged an exact timeline. John, though, is not entirely certain if these are man-made events or if they are of natural catastrophic devastation. The entities only seem to show John that in which they want to share with him; they are the ones in control at all times during a telepathic conversation, and this is not usually a two-way thing.

They have, interestingly, shared the technicalities of how their craft functions, and John, having a science background, was able to absorb scientific data far more easily than the average abductee. His interaction with them has mainly been associated with the small grey entities, but he has also seen humanoid and reptilian beings under certain circumstances.

During one encounter onboard the craft, John asked one of the beings which planet they originated from but did not get a direct answer. They have told him, however, that their race is several thousand years old, of which John intuitively estimated to be around ten thousand. They have also spoken about several other species visiting Earth, and that the planet is very important to many of them in that there is an abundance of resources here for them to utilize and benefit from. This also includes resources on the moon.

Too, the beings have shared information with John that habitable planets are not that uncommon in the universe. But they advise that planets similar to Earth, teaming with life and with millions of different species, are *not* common at all, and that there are only four or five similar planets in our galaxy to be this way. John distinctly remembers them telling him that they use time travel, but don't like to use it too frequently as it is far more dangerous than space travel itself. If used incorrectly, they could end up on an alternate timeline.

On one occasion while onboard their craft, John was taken to the dark side of the moon. He was told about a network of underground bases in this particular location that are occupied by the beings themselves, and that it is here where they build their space craft. It's interesting to note that many other abductees and experiencers alike have also spoken openly about being taken to the moon.

Renowned remote viewer Ingo Swann has written about seeing alien bases on the moon during his remote viewing sessions in his book *Penetration – The Question of Extraterrestrial and Human Telepathy.* During the session, he was given certain Moon coordinates that each represented specific locations on the moon's surface. What he remotely saw were towers, machinery, lights of different colors, and strange-looking buildings. He was also able to see bridges, though he could not figure out their purpose, one of which apparently just arched out and never connected to anywhere. Swann also mentions seeing domes of various sizes, round objects like saucers that displayed windows, and some objects that were huge and sitting next to craters or situated in caves. Others could be seen that appeared to be in something similar to air-field hangars. At one point, he was able to see some kind of "people" busy at work on something that Ingo could not identify.

It's important to note here that John is not the only abductee to have visited the dark side of the moon while being escorted by non-human entities aboard their craft. As mentioned, there are a number of abduction cases reported where others have stated that they, too, had frequented the moon. They have witnessed strange anomalies (as described by remote viewer Ingo Swann) and communication from the beings to some abductees has been one in which they have talked about their involvement with various moon projects.

Alien Encounters

"All at once, two small spheres came from the object. They made a sound as their spikes moved over the earth. They came to a stop beside him, grabbing his trousers, and began to drag him back to the UFO. The spiked objects were very similar to the UFO, only smaller. Taylor could smell a strong, sickening odor. He lost consciousness. When he regained consciousness, the spheres were gone, but his red setter was still there. The dog was panicky, running around and barking. Taylor tried to calm him down, but found that his voice was gone. He was very weak, and when he tried to stand, he couldn't. He crawled for a time until he was able to stand again."

~Author B.J. Booth

Excerpt: 1979 – *Dechmont Woods-Abduction of Robert Taylor*

Alice's Encounter Southern California

Experiencer/Abductee

Alice was aware that a number of unusual occurrences had taken place in her life while growing up, beginning when she was just two years old. An odd incident happened when she lived in Venice, California, and although she herself cannot consciously remember the specifics of the incident being so young, her mother recalled that one day as Alice was playing outside with her four-year-old neighbor and being watched intently by Alice's mother, the telephone rang and her mother stepped inside the house to answer it. After the short phone call had finished, she came back outside to the children and saw that Alice was nowhere to be seen. Her mother asked Alice's friend where she had gone, to which the four year old replied that she had taken her to the park and had left her there!

Alice's mother was frantic! She didn't know how to drive and there was no way that she could immediately go to get her. How was it possible that a four year old and a two year old could make their own way to the park? Coincidentally, a neighbor just happened to be driving along the Pacific Coast Highway (PCH) and noticed Alice standing by the bus stop crying. The neighbor picked her up straight away and took her back home to her mother. The strange thing about this incident was that the Pacific Coast Highway is an extremely busy long stretch of road, and there was absolutely no way that two young children could have crossed it safely by themselves, nor arrive to the park and back in time for Alice's mother to have finished her short phone conversation. The incident didn't make any sense.

Later in Alice's life, and being aware of a number of strange events including episodes of missing time and alien encounters, she came to the conclusion that from the early age of two, alien beings were interacting with her and were responsible for her disappearance that day. Upon reflection, she felt that her four-year-old friend had been "programmed" by these beings to say that they had gone to the park, and that she had left her there in order to cover up the real explanation of her missing time.

Later when Alice's family moved to Reseda, California, another incident occurred. She recalls the neighbors talking about a UFO sighting in the area and witnessing a strange, white substance referred to as "Angel Hair" that had fallen from the craft, covering two blocks of the neighborhood. Military personnel made a visit to the area, and took a few samples of the strange material before it quickly disappeared, followed by an interview with a witness that morning who was the driver of a bakery truck. Many years later as an adult, Alice discovered an article written by the well-known UFO author and researcher, Preston Dennett, who had written about this very incident of Angel Hair being found in the Reseda area, and a man from the military interviewing the owner of a bakery truck. At the time of the incident, Alice's father owned a bakery truck. She believed that it definitely had to be her father who was interviewed as he was the only person with such a truck in the area, and yet he had never spoken to the family about the interview whatsoever.

Alice's parents did hold a personal belief in UFOs and their occupants, and one day, her father openly spoke about a particular daylight sighting of a UFO he had witnessed in the San Fernando Valley area of California – a metallic, cigar-shaped craft that had a number of windows along the side of it. Her mother also spoke openly about a strange object that was embedded under the skin in the calf of her leg, and repeatedly said how she had fallen down the stairs which had resulted in the object becoming deeply embedded. Yet there was no portal of entry showing how the object could have gotten inside. Alice and her siblings believed that this was the result of her mother having her own encounters with nonhuman entities.

Tim, Alice's younger brother, also remembers his first experience as a young child of seeing "gray people" as he looked out through the bars of his crib, only to see the entities looking back observing him. Alice's elder sister also had an odd experience when she was five years old. Just before going to her first day of kindergarten, she noticed that her mother had suddenly disappeared from inside the house, and was nowhere to be found! As her mother didn't drive, her father was the one taking her to school that morning, and at the very end of the day, she was waiting for her parents to collect her; they never came.

Extremely upset and crying, a stranger suddenly came walking by. He picked her up and took her to the school office, where the staff immediately called her parents. Her father eventually came to get her, and said that *all* of the clocks had stopped working in the house, and that they had been unaware of the time. When she arrived home, her mother acted very strangely towards her, showing no emotion whatsoever, nor asking how her first day at school had been. This was very odd behavior because her mother and father were very loving parents. Alice's sister talked about this particular incident with her siblings when they were much older, and came to the conclusion that their mother's disappearance was the result of her being taken by alien beings yet again.

Strange experiences continued to happen throughout Alice's life as she got older, and in 1994, she and a group of friends visiting the Coronado Island in San Diego, California, experienced an alien encounter that they were not going to easily forget.

Alice and her friend Vicky, Tim (Alice's brother) and his wife, Jacqueline, plus two other friends, Keith and his wife, Julie, all decided to attend a weekend UFO conference at the Hotel del Coronado in March 1994. Although the conference was being held at the Coronado hotel itself, Alice and her friends stayed at a small motel called *The Village Inn*, an old Spanish-style building that had only fifteen rooms, three stories, and was built in 1928. They arrived at the motel on a Friday during torrential rain, as the conference was to commence the following day. Keith and Julie were given the room next to Alice and Vicky, while Tim and Jacqueline stayed in a room facing the front of the motel.

During this particular weekend, President Clinton and his wife, Hillary, were also arriving at Coronado Island to stay with friends at a beautiful private residence, not too far away from the Hotel del Coronado itself. The property boasted trails of luscious Ivy around the house, a large gate at the entrance, and was only two blocks away from the motel, where Alice could see the street on which the President was staying from her room. Due to the President's upcoming arrival, the entire area was completely guarded and monitored by the Secret Service.

After Alice and Vicky had unpacked their belongings and settled in their room, Alice joined her brother and his wife for a little shopping. Her friend, Vicky, decided to have regression therapy with the well-known regression therapist, Yvonne Smith, who was staying at the Hotel del Coronado and hosting the UFO conference. Vicky wanted to undergo regression so that she could uncover certain missing time episodes she couldn't account for, as well as vague memories of her alien encounters that she couldn't fully recall consciously. After Vicky had finished her regression, at around 7:30 p.m., she, Alice, and friend Yvonne made their way downstairs to have dinner.

The restaurant was situated in a beautiful large ballroom, where approximately three to four waiters were standing around each dinner table. They thought this to be strange that so many waiters should be present, as there were not a lot of people in the restaurant that night, and all three ladies were eating lightly, only having salads for dinner instead of three-course meals. The ladies became quickly aware that these "waiters" were not actually waiters at all, but Secret Service agents in disguise, who stood at a short distance of only seven feet or so behind their own table, talking into their sleeves and listening to their conversation about Vicky's regression. In fact, they noticed that many of the Secret Service agents were present throughout the entire hotel that weekend, obviously securing the area for President Clinton's visit.

Halfway through dinner, Vicky developed a headache and decided that she would go back to the motel room to take medication for it. When she eventually came back to Alice and Yvonne, she mentioned that she had been closely followed by a man in a dark suit. It was now approximately 9 p.m., and as dinner was now finished, both Alice and Vicky decided that they would walk back to the motel to go to bed. Again, they were followed by a man in a dark suit. Alice and Vicky would suddenly stop walking, and see that the dark-suited man would do exactly the same at precisely the same time. As they approached the corner before the motel and were approximately forty feet from the motel door, the man turned off and went in a different direction. They both knew that they were being closely watched by the Secret Service agents and felt extremely uncomfortable. But it was not only their group that was being closely followed; many other people were being watched in the area as well.

When they arrived inside the motel, they met Keith and his wife, Julie, in the lobby area who had just checked in. They mentioned that they would knock on Alice and Vicky's door the next morning to wake them up for breakfast. The ladies agreed that would be a good idea and then made their way up to the room. Alice was the first one to fall asleep, followed by Vicky who sat watching television for awhile. Vicky slept in the bed by the large window overlooking the side car park, while Alice took the other twin bed close to the door. That night, Alice recalled having some kind of a nightmare, and remembered seeing the intensity of a bright light entering the room – so bright that she could see it through her closed eye lids. The next thing she knew, it was morning, and that her blanket was wrapped around her neck like a scarf!

What transpired that night was very disturbing and shocking. The bright light that Alice experienced had actually come through the window between the hours of 1 a.m. and 2 a.m., followed by a number of four-foot-tall grey alien entities who floated through the *closed* window, and was witnessed by Vicky, who was then awake. The light was so intense that Alice started to awaken. Vicky watched as the beings floated past her and headed straight towards Alice who was now awake. Seeing them, Alice quickly jumped out of bed and ran towards the door, crouching in a corner crying and extremely upset. The entities had a terrible odor, similar to that of sulfur (which has been reported many times by experiencers). Vicky knew that they did not have any interest in her whatsoever and ignored her completely as if she didn't exist. (Vicky has had many encounters throughout her life, but her encounters are not specifically with the grey entities, but in particular, has experienced encounters with the *praying mantis*-type beings.)

The next thing that Vicky witnessed was Alice being floated out of the closed window, accompanied by the grey entities. She was in complete shock to what she was witnessing. Vicky felt totally helpless and even responsible for what had happened, as she had told Alice a week or so before arriving at Coronado Island, that whenever she takes a vacation, she always seems to experience an alien encounter and is often taken from her surroundings. Alice had reassured her that they would be fine and brushed it off, telling her that nothing like that would happen. But it had.

Within moments of Alice being taken through the closed window, Vicky heard a man scream in the hallway and knew that it was Keith. The beings did not stop at taking Alice that night, but had also come for Keith in the next room who, with extreme fear, ran out into the hallway. Tim's wife, Jacqueline, was also taken that night, and shockingly watched as a number of grey beings entered their room and physically floated Jacqueline up through the ceiling and into the disc-shaped craft that was awaiting above the motel. The entities had switched Tim off completely. He could do nothing to stop them, nor help Jacqueline in any way. He was totally helpless.

After Alice had been taken, Vicky understandably did not sleep at all that night; she was too afraid to sleep because she didn't know if Alice was going to be brought back. But during the early hours of the morning, somewhere around 4 a.m., she saw Alice being returned to the room through the closed window from which she had initially left, and was *floated* back into bed. In the morning, Alice felt quite ill and didn't feel like her usual self, having pains in her stomach and a very bad headache. She had no conscious memory of what had happened the night before. Alice just assumed that she wasn't feeling well because of the nightmare that she had, but did remember seeing the bright light through her closed eyelids. Other than that, she remembered nothing more. Vicky was afraid to tell her what had happened, and kept the experience to herself.

That morning, Keith knocked on Alice's door to see if she and Vicky were ready for breakfast. Alice explained that she wasn't feeling well,

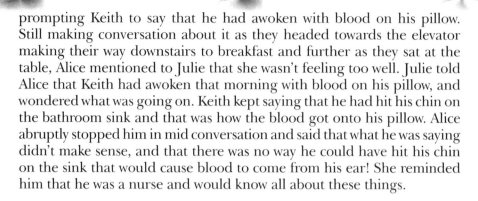

prompting Keith to say that he had awoken with blood on his pillow. Still making conversation about it as they headed towards the elevator making their way downstairs to breakfast and further as they sat at the table, Alice mentioned to Julie that she wasn't feeling too well. Julie told Alice that Keith had awoken that morning with blood on his pillow, and wondered what was going on. Keith kept saying that he had hit his chin on the bathroom sink and that was how the blood got onto his pillow. Alice abruptly stopped him in mid conversation and said that what he was saying didn't make sense, and that there was no way he could have hit his chin on the sink that would cause blood to come from his ear! She reminded him that he was a nurse and would know all about these things.

That morning Alice's brother, Tim, suddenly mentioned to the group out of the blue that he was not going to attend the conference, and said that he was going to take Jacqueline and Julie shopping instead. Alice asked why the sudden decision to not attend after he had paid the conference fee, but Tim was adamant that he was going nowhere near the Hotel del Coronado, whatsoever. The group couldn't understand what was wrong and why his sudden decision, and so only the three of them – Alice, Vicky and Keith – attended the conference that day without the others. The next morning, they all left to make the trip home.

It wasn't until many months later that they actually discovered the truth about what had happened to them that night at The Village Inn on Coronado Island. Vicky finally shared with Alice what she had witnessed in the room, which prompted them both to decide to undergo hypnotic regression with Yvonne Smith, who had hosted the conference that weekend in March. Even though Vicky underwent regression, she still had a considerable amount of conscious memory of Alice's encounter that night.

Alice had tried regression therapy on two separate occasions to uncover what she had experienced unconsciously, but Yvonne unfortunately had to end the session half way both times because Alice developed extremely painful headaches and was blocked from going any further.

Tim, Alice's brother, also had regression, and under hypnosis described what he saw that night. He recalled how nonhuman grey entities entered the hotel room and how they had physically taken his wife up through the ceiling. He'd watched in total disbelief how they manipulated her physical body in such a way that it allowed her to *effortlessly* pass through the solid structure of the ceiling. That the beings had somehow "switched him off," and that he was unable to move to do anything other than watch them take her, was horrifying.

Yvonne Smith was aware that there were eleven other individuals that particular weekend who had also experienced alien encounters at various hotels in the Hotel del Coronado area. They had all been frantic and in fear at what they were seeing, running down the corridors of the hotels not knowing what to do, and totally shaken to their core. The question was raised: How could these events have taken place when the neighborhood was completely guarded and patrolled by Secret Service men? Did these entities prevent the guards and the Secret Service from being conscious and "switched them off" too? Were these beings staging the whole event to show exactly what they were capable of doing? Alice couldn't help but to wonder if the Secret Service knew what had happened to them that night, and if the event was perhaps documented and classified in some government building.

Shortly after the strange experience Keith had at the Village Inn, he arranged to see a doctor regarding the continued problems with his ear. The doctor asked Keith what he had been using to prod deep inside his ear, and verified that his ear drum was badly punctured! This experience is not the only one of its kind for Keith; he has had numerous alien encounters over the years and has experienced a number of ill effects from the abductions. He and his wife have experienced alien encounters and abductions both growing up and as adults, but did not consciously realize it at the time. They had no memories of their experiences, other than repeated episodes of missing time.

Approximately a month or two after attending the conference, Alice discovered a strange "scoop" mark on her left leg. While getting ready for bed one night, she clearly heard a voice tell her to check her leg. Alice was not prone to hearing voices, and had never heard the voice before, but upon hearing it, immediately looked down at her leg, and sure enough, she saw a weird looking "kidney-shaped" scar on her calf. The scar was extremely irritating to look at, and she repeatedly tried to scratch it off her leg, so much so that she would continuously make it bleed.

Alice's Implant Removal Surgery

In 1996, Dr. Roger Leir took an x-ray of Alice's scar and pointed out to her that it was in fact not just a scar, but that there was some type of an object under the skin. He asked Alice how she felt about the object and if she would prefer to leave it be or have it removed. She said that she would prefer to have it removed. At the time, Dr. Leir had managed to access private funding for three implant surgeries. One involved a woman named Dolly who also had an object in the calf of her leg; a second surgery involved a patient who had an object in his jaw, and Alice's surgery would be the third.

> The well-known author of the book *Communion*, Whitley Streiber, was initially Dr. Leir's third patient, as he had also experienced alien encounters and, apparently, had an object in his ear lobe. But at the last minute, he'd decided to withdraw from the surgery as he felt that removing it would somehow affect his health. It's surprising how many experiencers do have similar thoughts when confronted about removing an object; it's as if they are programmed to think that way, and that they will suffer illness and certain consequences if they choose to interfere with it and have it removed.

Prior to Alice's surgery, she underwent a complete psychological profile. The diagnosis showed her to be normal and satisfactory. The unusual object was confirmed by a CAT scan and this particular area of skin had been subjected to high amounts of UV radiation. How does an ordinary housewife have a tiny area of her skin exposed to UV radiation, when the rest of her body has not been exposed? Furthermore, there was no evidence of inflammation, and no evidence of the body reacting to the foreign object in any way.

During the surgery, Dr. Leir turned over the layer of skin exposing the object. It was a small, milky-colored round object that looked identical to Dolly's, and was more biological in form than the other implant that was removed from the patient's jaw. These biological implants had a membrane around them that was extremely difficult to cut through. Numerous tests were done on them, and what was discovered was that Alice's implant contained *nano-tubes* and *nano-tube fibres* running through it! Nano-tubes are a relatively new technology, and were certainly not known as early as 1996. Some of the newest objects that Dr. Leir has removed have also displayed *deep space radio waves* in them, and are a fairly recent find in that some have displayed certain *frequencies*.

Alice believes that *whoever* these nonhuman entities were, they had taken a scoop out of the skin to somehow break the skin down into finer particles to securely encase the object so that the body did not reject it. It's important to point out also how the majority of experiencers feel a "new sense of freedom" once the object has been removed. But for Alice, she didn't feel that way; she felt extremely weak and almost passed out when the object was extracted.

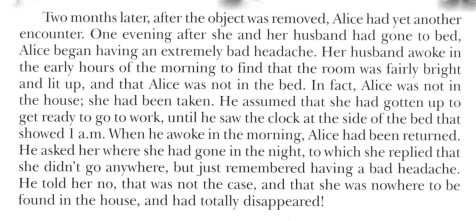

Two months later, after the object was removed, Alice had yet another encounter. One evening after she and her husband had gone to bed, Alice began having an extremely bad headache. Her husband awoke in the early hours of the morning to find that the room was fairly bright and lit up, and that Alice was not in the bed. In fact, Alice was not in the house; she had been taken. He assumed that she had gotten up to get ready to go to work, until he saw the clock at the side of the bed that showed 1 a.m. When he awoke in the morning, Alice had been returned. He asked her where she had gone in the night, to which she replied that she didn't go anywhere, but just remembered having a bad headache. He told her no, that was not the case, and that she was nowhere to be found in the house, and had totally disappeared!

Some days later, Alice slowly began to have recollections of being taken that particular night, and that during the encounter, believes that the beings realized that the object had been removed from her left leg, and that they were not happy about it. So they placed another implant in her ear, and when they returned her back to her home, she experienced considerable pain with it. Alice is of the opinion that even though experiencers have these objects removed, it does not mean that the encounters or abductions will stop. She has experienced the beings' frustration and annoyance first-hand when they found out that their objects have been tampered with. Sometimes these beings will even remove the object themselves, if they feel that the person is going to remove it.

It's apparent that because numerous experiencers have come forward who have had such implants, that the same statements are made by them time and time again. They say that these entities repeatedly communicate to them that they are not to remove the object ever; and in some cases, have implied that doing so would invite certain repercussions to their actions. Is this perhaps why Whitley Streiber did not have his implant removed from his ear lobe, after feeling that it would affect his health once doing so? However, some abductees who have had the objects removed have not met with said annoyances from the entities, nor in some cases have been re-implanted. It's uncertain as to why these non-human entities re-act in this way with some abductees and not others. It's all about what the beings want and their own agenda; it's what they want to achieve from it. It has been stated that there is the possibility that we are dealing with a number of different grey species, that may each have their own agenda when it comes to implants.

Alien Encounters

"The UFO came to a stop about seventy feet away. Moody could hear a high-pitched humming sound. He noticed a rectangular window in the craft through which he could see shadows resembling human forms. The next thing he would remember was seeing the object rising up into the sky and disappearing into the distance. Over the next few weeks, he was able to piece together an almost complete picture of the events. According to Moody's subsequent recollection, after being overcome by numbness, he had observed two beings approaching his car. About six feet tall, the creatures wore skintight black clothing. After a brief scuffle with them, he was rendered unconscious. He awoke on a slab inside the craft. His limbs felt leaden and immovable. Next to him stood the alien leader."

~www.ufocasebook.com

Excerpt:: *Abduction of Air Force Sergeant Charles L. Moody, 1975*

Tim's Encounter
Colorado

Experiencer/Abductee

Having experienced a number of very strange incidents over the past twenty-seven years, Tim is adamant, through these experiences, that we are not the only intelligent life in the universe.

Tim is happily married to his wife, Janet, and is a native of Yuma, Colorado. He was forty years old when he experienced his first alien encounter in 1978. During that year, in April, Tim had an intense and vivid dream that he was involved in a horrible car accident. Precisely one week later, he and his friend Ken were driving along the highway when Tim realized that he was actually living out a precognitive dream.

A few seconds later, the car suddenly hit an embankment and began to roll five times. The severe impact from the first roll had broken Tim's neck and fractured his spine. His friend traveling with him desperately helped Tim out of the vehicle that was now in the embankment, and managed to waive down a passing vehicle for help.

He was then taken to the nearest hospital to be treated for his severe injuries. The doctor told Tim that he probably would never walk again, and as a result of the horrific accident, would be a quadriplegic for the rest of his life. But Tim was unwavering with the doctor saying that this wasn't going to happen. He told the doctor that he would make a full recovery. During his hospitalization and while under sedation, Tim had yet another strange dream, a recollection that he had encountered a UFO.

Months later, Tim did make a successful and complete recovery from his injuries, and on May 30, 1978 at approximately 11p.m., Tim and his wife, Janet, were driving on a lonely and desolate road, returning home from a medical checkup earlier that day in Denver. While driving along the highway, Tim saw a large dimly lit object appear and pass in front of the car. He continued to watch it as it descended behind a hill, only to re-emerge moments later.

Tim described how the object moved away and then detoured back towards them somewhat, and that it was totally silent. He also noticed two bright lights that shone at the back of the craft. Backing up his car a little, he could see that the object had moved to the west of them, gradually coming closer as it passed underneath the power and telephone lines, eventually landing in a field.

The object was approximately a hundred feet long and around twenty feet wide. Janet, who happened to be five months pregnant at the time with their first child, just sat and stared at the object, not believing what she was seeing. After a few moments of watching the object, they decided that they should drive on towards the town and head home. Tim and his wife have no conscious memory of being taken onboard the craft that night, but Tim states that he felt an odd feeling just before continuing to drive from the scene.

Twenty years later, in 1998, while working at a construction job, Tim accidentally struck his thumb with a hammer. The pain from the blow was so excruciating that he thought he had badly fractured his finger, and so he went to the emergency room at Yuma clinic. After the doctor had suggested they take an x-ray, the doctor noticed that there was a piece of metal in Tim's wrist and asked him if he knew anything about it. At that very moment, Tim's mind began to race; he knew immediately what the object in his wrist was, and associated it with the missing time that he and Janet experienced in 1978, while witnessing the UFO.

Tim never really had an interest in the subject of UFOs or alien encounters before his own experiences, and was certainly not aware of the so-called alien implants that were being discovered in many people's bodies. But after seeing his own x-ray and the evidence that it showed of the metal object, Tim explored the internet to learn more information about the subject and joined an on-line encounter support group.

It was in this group that he heard about Dr. Roger Leir, a successful podiatrist who was at the forefront in removing these strange objects reported to be "alien implants." Tim contacted Dr. Leir about his own UFO encounters, and in particular the strange-looking piece of metal that the x-ray revealed to be in his wrist.

Tim came to the decision that he wanted the object removed, and so Dr. Leir arranged for the surgery to be performed on February 5, 2000. This particular surgery was the ninth for Dr. Leir, and was performed at a medical facility in Thousand Oaks, California, along with a second doctor.

What was removed from Tim's left wrist was a small "melon seed" -type implant, which was approximately 2.8 inches (7cm) long and 1.5 inches (4cm) wide. There was a dark area that revealed a metal core, and when a magnet was placed in close proximity to the object, it literally leapt to the magnet! Dr. Leir's analysis of this object revealed that it contained carbon nano-tubes, indicating that it possessed extraterrestrial material. There were no known earthly isotopes found within the object, and it was a highly advanced form of technology.

Over the years, Tim has made two attempts to be hypnotically regressed. The second regression was with Dr. Leo Sprinkle, a very well-known hypnotherapist in the state of Colorado. He was able to regress Tim to the point where the bright lights appeared on the craft, but then amnesia quickly set in and Tim could not go forward. Dr. Sprinkle tried every method possible to get Tim past the point of seeing the bright lights, but with no success. This process alone took forty-five minutes, and as Tim could go no further, Dr. Sprinkle brought him out of the hypnotic state. As soon as Tim came to and was aware of his surroundings, he began complaining terribly about his eyes, and looking in the mirror saw that the schlera of the eye was covered with blood, and were tearing profusely. It was as if he had literally been looking at an intense bright light, full on, for forty-five minutes, and was left uncontrollably wiping his eyes!

Unfortunately, Tim has never been able to go beyond the point of seeing the two bright lights on the craft during his regression therapy, making this yet another example of how these beings *block* or *suppress* the memories of the encounter.

Tim has always been very open and matter-of-fact about his UFO experiences, as well as the object that was removed from his wrist. This is actually quite rare, as many experiencers and abductees are reluctant to come forward due to fear of ridicule from others who are not so open of such a phenomena.

Like Alice's regression therapy, Tim also had problems getting past a certain point of his UFO/abduction experience while under hypnosis. It seems that it is this way for a number of experiencers who have also tried to uncover the truth of what happened to them beyond a certain point. Quite often, the experiencer is met with physical pain as they approach the proverbial brick wall, usually in the form of a severe headache that continues until the experiencer is finally brought out of the hypnosis state. It's concluded by many regression therapists that these beings do not want the experiencer to remember the whole experience for whatever reason, either at all, or not until some point in the near future when they feel it is right to do so.

Alien Encounters

"All...of them wore a very tight-fitting siren-suit, made of soft, thick, unevenly striped grey material. This garment reached right up to their necks where it was joined to a kind of helmet made of a grey material that looked stiffer and was strengthened back at nose level. Their helmets hide everything except their eyes, which were protected by two round glasses, like the lenses in ordinary glasses. Through them, the men looked at me, and their eyes seemed to be much smaller than ours, though I believe that may have been the effect of the lenses. All of them had light-colored eyes that looked blue to me, but this I cannot vouch for. Above their eyes, those helmets looked so tall that they corresponded to what the double of the size of a normal head should be."

~Author Terry Melanson – 2001

Excerpt: Antonio Villas Boas Abduction Episode
Ground Zero

Patricia's Encounter
Western United States

Experiencer/Abductee

Patricia was a twenty-three-year-old married woman, eight months pregnant, and the mother of two small boys, ages five and six years old, when she encountered her first UFO experience in 1969. During the month of October that particular year, Patricia and her husband, John, had thought about taking a vacation, as he had been working extremely long hours, and most especially as the new baby would soon be born. It seemed an excellent opportunity to take a small break before their new arrival.

After taking a few days to decide where they might take their vacation, John had suggested the idea of a fishing trip at a beautiful, rural location in the state of Texas. Patricia thought it was a great idea, especially for the kids, as they would experience a fun camping trip and help their dad catch fish!

They studied a map to pin-point the exact location and the best route to take for their trip, penciling in scheduled stops along the way so that they could rest properly. Within a day or two of preparing all of the cooking equipment, food, and camping gear, they started to load what they needed into the car and were ready to head off on their trip.

During the drive, Patricia noticed that the journey was taking much longer than expected. The time was 4:30 p.m., and, as yet, they had still not arrived at their destination. Some of the roads were not marked clearly, and by then it was evident that the map they were using was not an up-to-date one. Patricia then noticed what she thought was possibly a building in the distance; it was in fact an old iron bridge that crossed a beautiful stream, and where the campsite could be seen beyond it.

The camp site was in close proximity to the river with a few trees and bushes surrounding it. As soon as John had parked the car, everyone got out and started to unpack before it got too dark. John prepared the tent, while Patricia gathered together the food and pots and pans for cooking. After preparing the tent, John and the boys went searching for firewood to be ready to cook the meal.

Darkness began to descend, and the children remembered that they had packed their flashlights and ran to the car to get them. Finding a comfortable log to sit on, they started to flash their lights towards the sky. Only a few stars were visible.

The kids quickly shouted for their mother to come over to them, as they had something to show her. There was a brighter-than-usual star, and one of the boys gave a couple of flashes with his "torch" towards it. In amazement, Patricia and John watched as the two flashes were returned! John ran back to the tent to grab a couple more larger and powerful flashlights. He gave one to Patricia, and pointed his upward towards the bright star, giving it two short flashes and one long flash. Within seconds, the flashes were returned again and in the same manor.

They couldn't believe what they were witnessing. Patricia began to turn her flashlight towards the "star" and gave a number of flashes herself, which were also returned. Within moments they noticed a few more "stars" moving in closer and accompanying the one they were flashing at.

After dinner, Patricia and her husband sat on a log by the crackling fire, while both children slept in their sleeping bags. John asked Patricia what she thought was going on with the weird lights that were flashing back at them. She said that she wasn't sure, but thought that it might be helicopters from a local airbase, fooling around with them for a bit of fun.

The next morning, John and the boys were excited to start their planned fishing which lasted for half of the day. Much later, all decided to go for a hike around the area to enjoy the outdoor scenery. After arriving back to the campsite early evening, John and the children collected more wood for the fire, while Patricia prepared to cook dinner.

Afterward, they all played a few games before going off to bed, and talked about what they might like to do the following day. John mentioned a really great area of the river where some of the biggest fish had been caught, so John and the children wanted to give it a try. The fire was burning pretty intensely as they went to bed that night (and was still burning when they awoke the next morning).

At around 1 a.m., Patricia was awakened quite abruptly by John. He stood over her in the tent, and with sheer terror on his face demanded for Patricia to immediately get up and to get the children and put them in the car. She wondered what could possibly be the problem and why John was acting strangely. She jumped up quickly from her sleeping bag and, in a panic, stumbled around the tent before getting the children. John peered back into the tent and again asked her to hurry.

She quickly grabbed one of the boys abruptly as he slept in his sleeping bag, which suddenly awakened him and made him cry. She told him that everything was okay and to go back to sleep as she lay him in the back of the car. John followed behind carrying the other son who was still fast asleep in his arms.

Patricia abruptly asked John what was going on, and why he wanted them to suddenly leave from the vacation. He answered her in a very curt tone, and asked her not to ask any more questions but to just get in the car. Within moments, they were driving off down the desolate, dark road, leaving all of their camping equipment behind. Patricia, who was now becoming more and more angry and annoyed, demanded to know what had happened. John told her that he had seen *something* under the bridge. She asked him what he meant, and if he was referring to having seen people or animals, to which John abruptly answered *no*!

Driving further down the very dark and narrow road with only the car headlights illuminating the way, they were heading back towards the bridge, the way they had come. John suddenly asked Patricia to look behind them, and if she could see a bright light following. She acknowledged that she could see it, to which John said that maybe it was just a truck that was behind them. After glancing back to look for a second time, Patricia saw that the light was now getting brighter and brighter and catching up with them.

It was becoming more apparent that this brightly lit object was definitely *not* a truck, and the sheer enormous size of it would most certainly not fit on the bridge! As they approached the bridge and were just about to cross over the other side of it, Patricia's attention was focused at the front of the car. John now seemed to be in some kind of a "switched off" or "zombie-like" state as Patricia was yelling for him to stop the car. The vehicle came to an abrupt halt, and as it did, both looked at each other totally dumbfounded.

Once they managed to gather themselves, Patricia asked what had just happened. John had no idea, and just kept staring through the windshield. The odd thing was that they noticed that the car was now facing in the **opposite** direction from the way they had just been heading. They were in fact heading back towards the campsite!

John drove furiously back over the old iron bridge, and, as they approached the campsite, Patricia was concerned that there was something very weird about the whole thing. What had just happened to them made no sense whatsoever, and as they arrived back at the campsite, Patricia noticed that the campfire was completely out! She couldn't understand how that could have happened, as John had made the fire to last throughout the whole night until the morning hours – they had literally only been gone for a few minutes. However, hours of time had just totally disappeared. They stared at each other trying to make sense of the whole strange event, and decided that they should perhaps just go home.

As they drove back, Patricia remained silent, and observed a greenish light following them. She was afraid to say anything about it to John, but realized he must have seen it also. The object continued to follow them for a number of miles and never wandered from its path.

The greenish light kept a steady pace behind them all the way home, and after eventually turning onto the main highway, John drove to a maximum speed where the light eventually disappeared. It was 7 a.m. when they finally arrived home, and they were very happy to see it. They felt that they could finally put their weird experience behind them, or so they thought. Little did Patricia know that her experiences would continue.

The following day, Patricia had a scheduled appointment with her obstetrician to check on her pregnancy, and to make sure that the baby's development was sound. Although Patricia was concerned for the baby after the traumatic experience she'd had on the camping trip, the examination proved that all was well. Her baby daughter was healthy and was born on schedule.

To date, Patricia mentions that Sonya, her daughter, is extremely intuitive and has a very high IQ. She has also developed a real talent for writing, and experiences a number of premonitions, as well as having some uncanny abilities. Patricia also states how "different" Sonya is from her other two children.

Patricia's Continued Experiences

A year later, in 1970, Patricia and John were lying in bed. It was approximately 12:05 a.m. when Patricia finally stopped reading her book for the night, switched off the light, and went to sleep.

Around 3 a.m., she was awoken by a strange green light surrounding the bed. She looked around the room to see where the light was coming from, and realized that it was actually outside the window. She noticed, too, that she couldn't move any part of her body. Even so, she tried desperately to wake John, but could not. He seemed, once again, to be in a "switched off" mode.

After some time had lapsed, Patricia was able to move her body, but as she moved her head, she saw that she was no longer in her bedroom. Rather, she was in a strange-looking huge room, somewhere else. She found herself sitting on a table in a room with odd-looking beings all around her. Her hands were the only part of her body that she could not move as they were being held by the beings that were to the sides of her.

Continuing to look around, she became aware of three huge transparent cylinders, which looked like they were made of glass and approximately eighteen feet tall. Inside each one of these cylinders was an object about the size of a basketball that was making a weird motion-like noise. Each tube had what looked like a twisted fan belt that formed a complete moving strip. The basketball size objects seemed to be in perpetual motion, and Patricia noticed that a sound similar to the wind was coming from inside the cylinders.

Patricia also noticed that she was very high up, about thirty feet above the cylinders and on some kind of a balcony. She thought to herself that if she was to fall from this height she would be dead instantly. Looking down below, she could see various equipment and other working parts. Then, the next thing she remembered was suddenly being back in her bed. She tried to wake her husband by shouting his name, who, this time, woke up immediately with a frightened expression on his face. He asked Patricia what was going on and where the green light was coming from, but within moments and before Patricia could answer, a "humming" sound filled the bedroom, and at the same time sounded like it was coming from outside and above the house. Shortly, the greenish light started to fade, and the room turned back to its prior darkness.

Patricia's Implant Removal Surgery

In 1995, Patricia had an x-ray taken of her foot, due to a sliver of wood that had become embedded fairly deep underneath the skin. It was during this particular x-ray that two foreign objects became apparent in her left great toe; the x-ray showed that they were metallic!

Patricia was in denial about having these objects due to the fact that there was no scarification, or any portal of entry, to show where they had

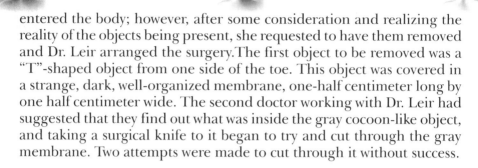

entered the body; however, after some consideration and realizing the reality of the objects being present, she requested to have them removed and Dr. Leir arranged the surgery. The first object to be removed was a "T"-shaped object from one side of the toe. This object was covered in a strange, dark, well-organized membrane, one-half centimeter long by one half centimeter wide. The second doctor working with Dr. Leir had suggested that they find out what was inside the gray cocoon-like object, and taking a surgical knife to it began to try and cut through the gray membrane. Two attempts were made to cut through it without success.

The second object to be removed was on the opposite side of the toe, and was similar to that of a small cantaloupe seed that also had a strange coating to it. Both of these objects did exhibit magnetic qualities, as determined by the GAUSS meter, which detects magnetic and electromagnetic fields, and in this case, read six mgauss on the meter. While Patricia felt no physical pain from having these strange objects in her toe, she did have psychological stress from seeing the initial x-ray.

Prior to, and after, the surgery, Dr. Leir arranged for Patricia to be examined by a psychologist. Once the objects were removed, Patricia told the psychologist that she was experiencing a "new found feeling of freedom." These are almost the exact words spoken by several other patients who have also had these strange objects removed by Dr. Leir and his team.

Dr. Leir, as mentioned earlier, has been a practicing Podiatrist for over forty-seven years, and at the time of this surgery, neither doctor had ever seen anything like these strange objects come out of a person's body. Interestingly enough, once the research was complete on Patricia's case, Dr. Leir was personally shown x-rays of Patricia's mother's foot before she had passed away, which astonishingly revealed that she too, like Patricia, also had the exact same two objects in *her* toe!

It's apparent that these non-human entities are concerned with choosing a person who has specific DNA characteristics to help them attain their mission. They are highly interested in family lineage and their gene pool. This is the case with Patricia and her mother, and other such abductees mentioned in the various chapters within the book. It's highly likely that Patricia's children might also be involved with the phenomena at some stage in their lives, especially Patricia's daughter, Sonia, who appears to show certain abilities and characteristics that these beings may have perhaps given to her in the first place.

Alien Encounters

"It's always the light that comes first, Then I see the tall one rise up at the foot of the bed. Suddenly there's lots of little ones everywhere. They're fuzzy and indistinct, and they move very fast. I can't move or speak, but I'm awake and I can see and hear and feel. I want to scream and run, but the sound doesn't come out and my body doesn't move. I hate them. I hate them, I have to go with them. They take me to an operating theatre, like at the hospital. It's all white and shiny. Sometimes it's a circular room with a metal floor. It's always cold. They're there. The big one touches me but I don't feel it, like as if I've had an anaesthetic."

~www.ufocasebook.com

Excerpt: *Abduction of Jason Andrews* – 1987

Paul's Encounter
Western United States

Experiencer/Abductee

Paul was only six years old when he experienced his first encounter with the unknown. He was an only child, and a typical farm boy who was responsible for various chores around the farm once he arrived home from the day at school, situated in a rural location.

His encounter began one night after his mother had securely tucked him into bed early. Sometime during the middle of the night he suddenly awoke from a sound sleep, after hearing a voice in his head telling him to get out of bed, get dressed, and to make his way outside to the front porch. He felt as if he had no control over his body and that some unknown force was controlling him. He got out of bed, got dressed, and walked out the bedroom door, down the hallway, and onto the front porch, where he gazed into the darkness of the night sky and the beauty of the full moon sitting in the heavens.

It was an extremely cold night, but Paul didn't seem to notice the outside temperature whatsoever, nor that his bare feet were touching the cold ground beneath him. He felt compelled to walk around the back of the house, guided by this inexplicable force. He then wandered into a field that he had plowed earlier that day with his father, looked straight up into the crisp, clear night sky and was amazed to see a collection of beautiful lights, a *show* of lights that moved back and forth. His eyes became transfixed on a particular light that left the group, and made its way slowly toward him. It was a ball of light, larger than the size of a basketball that got closer and closer to him.

Now standing completely still, his fear began to grow as the object came closer and stopped only eighteen feet from him. Staring at it intensely, he reached out to grab the ball of light that now began to suddenly spin and made a hissing sound as it did so. Once again, he was unable to move his body as the unseen force held him rigid, all the time feeling his fear ultimately getting the better of him. His sheer willpower allowed him to break free from the strange force that was immobilizing him. He turned around and ran back to the house. As he did, he heard a loud explosion and felt an instant pain in the back of his left hand. At that point, Paul became unconscious and later came to with his mother holding him in her arms. He told his mother the whole story of what had happened that night, and his experience with the strange ball of light, but his father was less amused to hear about Paul's experience, and asked that he never talk about it again.

As Paul got older, he and his friends would tell stories of seeing strange craft hovering in the sky, and would tease each other about gazing up into the darkness for many, many hours, and playing practical jokes with one another that they were seeing UFOs. But a few years later, their pranks diminished as they would encounter the real thing!

In 1965, Paul and a friend decided to take a fishing trip to one of the local lakes, which proved to be quite uneventful, as the hopes of catching a number of fish that day didn't quite go to plan. Making their way back home that evening, Paul's friend glanced up through the windshield, and he asked Paul to look at the strange airplane that was flying over head.

Paul slowed the car and looked up to see if he could see it. Now approaching his house, he pulled into the driveway, and got out to take a better look. In doing so, he noticed the neighbors standing in the street looking upwards also. Paul curiously asked them what was going on. One of the neighbors immediately pointed to the sky, and said that the strange plane had been up there for two hours!

Both Paul and his friend were excited and intrigued about what they were witnessing and got back in the car to drive to a better place to observe the strange flying object. As they drove down the highway, Paul's friend decided to stick his head out of the window so that he wouldn't lose sight of it. They came to a dirt clearing off the highway and jumped out of the vehicle. They both realized that this was no ordinary craft, and quickly grabbed a flashlight, pointed it up to the sky, and flashed a couple of quick flashes at it.

Staring at the sky in amazement, the object flashed back! They flashed again and immediately had a signal returned to them. The craft now suddenly started to descend, moving slowly before hovering overhead. Paul signaled to the object once more, and again the craft responded. He knew that *whatever* or *whoever* was controlling the object had to be intelligent.

They stood underneath the circular craft transfixed as they looked up at the metallic structure. The center of the object displayed a large circle with three smaller circles within it, each emitting a bluish-green glow. They noticed a small opening in the middle of the craft where they realized the returned flashing light to be coming from, which had now changed its color to red. Fixing his gaze on the multitude of stars that surrounded the object as a valid reference point to the solid structure he was witnessing, Paul began to question his sanity and felt as though he was losing his mind.

The object was completely silent, and the air didn't seem to stir as it hovered in the night sky for approximately ten minutes or so. It gave off a real eerie feeling as it slowly drifted off across the sky, and Paul continued to acknowledge that this object was not from here, but from another world!

Paul and his friend, still curious, got back in the car and followed the object down the highway for as long as they could, and saw that the craft was heading toward the city. All of a sudden, the object immediately turned 180 degrees, heading back towards them. Paul quickly pulled off the road and stopped the car. As he did so, the object also stopped and hovered for a brief moment before taking off at lightening-like speed, disappearing into the night sky. Both boys sat and looked at each other in amazement and disbelief at what they had just witnessed. The reality of the experience was something that they would never forget.

In 1971, Paul lived in Venezuela, and at the time, had been involved in a car accident, leaving him with an injured left arm. During an examination, the physician thought it would be a good idea to have an x-ray of both his arm and hand, and Paul agreed.

The doctor asked Paul if he had ever injured his left hand, or possibly had surgery on it, to which Paul answered *no* and that he'd never undergone surgery either. The doctor then pointed to a small object on the x-ray and showed Paul that it was situated in his left hand. The doctor added further that it was a solid piece of metal of some kind and asked Paul if it caused any pain. Paul felt no discomfort from the object whatsoever, and so the doctor said that it was probably nothing to be concerned about – probably an old cyst. This was a very strange statement to make, as the x-ray showed the object to be definitively metallic... The conversation about his hand with the Doctor triggered a childhood memory for Paul, a memory of that strange night when he was a six-year-old boy, standing out in his father's potato field watching the ball of light.

Three years later, Paul had proposed marriage to his girlfriend, and together, they made a trip to Texas to share the good news with his parents. The get-together went very well, and Paul's parents totally accepted his fiancé. After the evening's conversation, and while driving back home, Paul's fiance was drawn to something odd in the sky, and pointed towards it, asking Paul what he thought the object was. He slowed the vehicle and looked upwards towards the sky, and was astonished to see a craft exactly the same as the one he and his friend had seen back in the '60s.

He decided to stop the vehicle, and noticed that as he did so, the craft began to descend directly toward them. His fiancé now became extremely afraid and upset, and began to scream. Paul reassured her that everything would be okay, and wondered if there were any other people who were also witnessing the object. He pressed firmly on the car horn in the hope that the neighbors would hear and could see the object, too. But as he rolled down the car window and pointed towards the object, it suddenly came to a halt, and then with an incredible burst of speed, it shot upwards directly into the night sky.

Paul's Implant Removal Surgery

Before Paul had the object removed, he took the fact quite lightly that he had an object in the back of his hand. He would often demonstrate to his friends by taking a stud finder and moving it over a certain area of his hand, and watching the object rise up, just for sheer fun. His friends would laugh and comment how they had never seen anything like it before, and Paul assured them that they never would see anything like it again!

The object had remained in Paul's body for forty-one years, never giving him any pain whatsoever, but he finally decided that he wanted to proceed in having it removed. This was Dr. Leir's second patient with a strange object in his body, and it was removed the very same day after Dr. Leir's other patient, Patricia, had her object removed.

Before performing the surgery, Dr. Leir arranged for Paul to talk with a psychologist, who listened to his experiences and analyzed his mental stability. Paul passed all of the necessary tests and questioning by the psychologist with flying colors, and the surgery was then scheduled to take place.

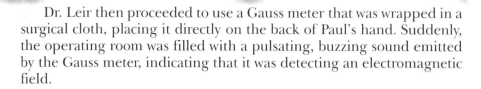

Dr. Leir then proceeded to use a Gauss meter that was wrapped in a surgical cloth, placing it directly on the back of Paul's hand. Suddenly, the operating room was filled with a pulsating, buzzing sound emitted by the Gauss meter, indicating that it was detecting an electromagnetic field.

As the doctors proceeded to remove the object, they realized, after one hour had passed and there was still no sign of the object, that this would be a slow and tedious effort. The object was much deeper in the hand than previously thought. They then had to use a certain device that would allow them to penetrate deeper into the tissue.

Once arriving at the location, a dark-colored object was now in the grasp of the surgical instrument. What was shocking about the object was that it was identical to the one that was removed during Patricia's surgery. It was shaped like a small cantaloupe seed and measured approximately .23 inches (6mm) in length by .0039 inches (0.1mm) in thickness. The object appeared to be covered with a grayish, shiny biological coating which was intimate with the metallic portion. Numerous pore like *sulci* (cavities) were seen on the surface of the object. The doctors tried to cut through it but without any success, just like the previous object they had removed from Patricia's toe.

Analysis of the object showed that the majority of it was composed of meteoric iron, and had a ceramic- and crystal-like outer structure to it. The object was highly magnetic with a magnetic field strength of 4 mil gauss. No radio frequencies were tested for at this time, and there was no isotopic ratio testing performed on either Paul's object or Patricia's.

As with so many of these strange objects found within people's bodies, they always seem to display the same type of characteristics again and again – gray, shiny biological coatings, and more often than not, metallic in nature. A number of implants recently removed have also shown to be highly magnetic, and not surprisingly, cannot be cut! It's truly mind-blowing how there is no scarification ever found on the surface of the abductee's skin; no portal of entry as to how these objects were ever implanted in the first place. Indeed, it seems very evident that a highly advanced form of technology is being utilized here to perform such an invasion of the body.

Photographs of Alleged Alien Implants

As Shown Through The Light Microscope

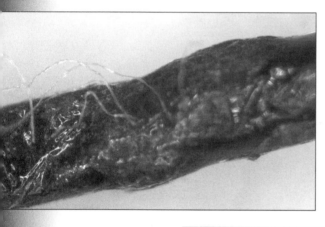

AST1T2B-40 Light Microscope Image – 40X Magnification Surgery #2 – Object removed from Paul's left hand

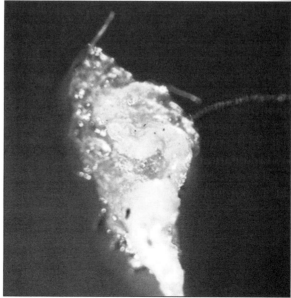

AL8-16-96 Light Microscope Image – 40X Magnification Surgery #4 – Object removed from Alice's left calf

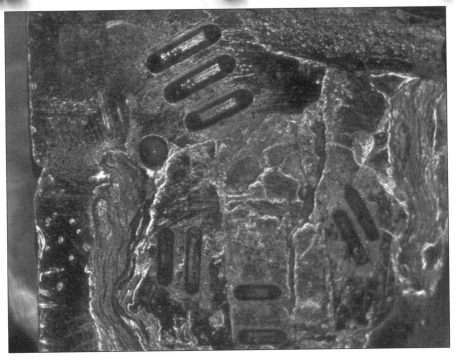

UT-Metal Cro   Light Microscope Image – 40X and 100X Magnification
Surgery #11 – Object removed from Tim's Wrist.

SC-080906-40x(2)   Light Microscope Image – 1X and 400X Magnification
Surgery #15 – Object removed from John's toe

Photographs provided by Steve Colbern and Dr. Roger Leir of A & S Research

Alien Encounters

"It was then I turned and saw a small grey being with his back turned doing something at a counter. I heard the clinking of metal against metal. I had only heard this when I was preparing my surgical instruments for my doctor in surgery. Then my guide asked me to go and sit down on the table in the middle of the room. I told him that I wouldn't do it and he said it would be much easier if I would comply. He was not smiling and I was scared. I did not want to be left in this room with this grey alien!"

~www.ufocasebook.com

Excerpt: *The Christa Tilton Story,* 1987
www.thewatcherfiles.com/dulce
/chapter25.htm

Tall White Extraterrestrials at Indian Springs, Nevada

Since the 1940s, the United States Army/Air Force established their training facility at Indian Springs, and it has been home for many military groups. Today, it is known as *Creech Air Force Base* after being renamed in 2005, when it was formerly known as *Indian Springs Air Force Auxiliary Air Field*. The base is located approximately thirty-five miles northwest of Las Vegas, and forty-five miles northwest of Nellis Air Force base. The area is named Indian Springs for the *artesian spring* that provides the locale with water.

It was here at the Air Force base between the years of 1965-1967 that retired Airman Charles Hall, claims that on several occasions, while serving at the Indian Springs ranges as a weather observer, he encountered an extraterrestrial race of beings known as the *Tall Whites*.

He was enlisted in the USAF in July 1964, where after completing his training at Lackland AFB in San Antonio, Texas, was then trained as a USAF weather observer at the USAF Weather Training School at Chanute AFB, Illinois. He was assigned to the weather squadron stationed at Nellis AFB at Las Vegas, Nevada, for two years between 1965 to 1967, and while permanently stationed there, was assigned as weather observer to the Nellis gunnery ranges located at Indian Springs, Nevada.

While at the gunnery ranges, he discovered that there was a base the U.S. Government maintained for a group of alien beings that he refers to as the *Tall Whites*, and details his encounters with them in his three-book trilogy entitled: *Millennial Hospitality*. Charles tells of how these Tall White beings often silently observed him, that they could freely come and go from the base, and were even present in the barracks, as well as in the weather shacks.

Over the years, Charles has given a number of interviews with various well-respected researchers regarding his personal encounters

Whites at Indian Springs, and in those interviews has personal opinion that these particular alien beings have ed here on Earth since the early 1950s, and could have quite possibly been based in Nevada for hundreds of years prior. Dr. Michael E. Salla, Ph.D, a pioneer in the development of "Exopolitics," the political study of extraterrestrial presence on Earth, is also of the belief that the Tall Whites were the race of beings that were associated with the much talked about 1954 meeting with President Eisenhower, and that they, in fact, established their base in the Indian Springs area of Nevada during that time.

It is claimed that their meeting with Eisenhower allowed the Tall Whites and the U.S. Government to have a technology exchange program. They were willing to share some of their technology with the U.S. Military if it was to their advantage to do so – those technologies being related to radio and communication systems – but would not divulge their technological secrets of how to build anti-gravity craft that could travel faster than the speed of light, or faster than various forms of advanced weaponry. We were simply not ready for such an advanced technology at that time. Charles also mentions that, over the years, he has witnessed their black triangular craft that uses an anti-gravity propulsion system, and is perfectly silent. He states that their ships are made from titanium, and are deep-space craft that travel faster than the speed of light. They also have their *so called* scout ships, which are white in color and assembled here on Earth; these are too small for crossing deep space. He further adds that the Tall Whites have no interest in dominating the Earth, nor taking over Governments, but simply want to maintain friendly liaisons with the U.S. Government so that they can continue to use the base.

Charles states that if you look straight north to the Indian Springs Valley and slightly to the east, you will see the location of their main base in the mountains, and that the location is known as Area 54. The beings' habitat is apparently underground to which there are a set of tunnels that lead to the entrances of their living area.

Physically, the Tall White beings are humanoid, thin and fragile, and are so called because of their skins' appearance, which is as white as a sheet of paper. They have white hair also, and quite high foreheads. Their eyes are twice as large as ours, blue in color with white pupils, and their ears and nose are approximately half the size of a human being's. They have no teeth, but only ridges as they are plant eaters, and are

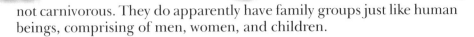

not carnivorous. They do apparently have family groups just like human beings, comprising of men, women, and children.

Charles claims that these extraterrestrials live to be around 700 years old, and that during their adult life, their height is around six feet tall, but once they reach the equivalent of middle age, they do become much taller. He recalls how one night at the base he saw an older Tall White being standing next to the control tower that was situated in an area at Range Three, and that the height of the being's head was parallel with one of the cross beams. The very next day, Charles went back to the location with a yardstick and measured the being's height to be eight and a half feet tall!

Throughout his presence at the base, he states that the beings never divulged their place of origin to him, but upon asking one of them where they had come from, a female being simply smiled and asked Charles if he was familiar with the names of the star systems, to which he replied that he was not. The female being answered that even if she was to tell him, that he would be non the wiser of their home location. Charles did mention, however, the star *Arcturus* to them, which is thirty-six light years away from Earth, and noticed that the beings became a little agitated upon hearing that name.

Charles makes reference to ancient Greek mythology dating to 972 B.C., noting that the star Arcturus was given the name the "watcher star," because the ancient Greeks claimed that when they were camping on warm Summer evenings, a group of tall white Gods would ascend from Arcturus and stand beyond the campfire watching them. For that reason, he believes that it is very probable that the Tall Whites have been visiting Earth for at least 3,000 years.

In his book, *Millennial Hospitality,* Charles describes three other military personnel who worked at the base during the same time period. Researcher and field investigator David Coote attempted to seek corroborating testimony from these three individuals who were stationed with Charles at Indian Springs Auxiliary Field. The result of his investigation makes it clear that although the testimony of the three witnesses was not conclusive, they were significant in firmly validating Charles' presence at the base as well as having information about various incidents talked about by the these military men and others.

What was confirmed during the interview was that all three men were employed as weather observers at the same time as Charles, and that they remembered him and acknowledged his presence at the base. They recalled their everyday duties and described the base just as Charles had written about in his trilogy. They also recalled names of various people who Charles had also mentioned.

The three witnesses were asked if they had read any of the books that Charles had written – none of the men had. David Cootes asked the men how well they knew Charles Hall, to which they replied that they knew him very well, and that he was an exceptionally nice guy, intelligent, and yet reserved. They also added that Charles spent more time out at the ranges than any of them ever had.

One of the men expressed that he and others constantly heard rumors about certain incidents at the base, that they believed Charles personal experiences wholeheartedly, and that he was indeed dealing with *something* out of the ordinary. One witness added that he personally never felt alone when he was out at the base, and went on to say that even the Air Police never responded to calls out at the ranges because they themselves were afraid.

The witness also stated to David Cootes that Charles and other base personnel used to talk about an urban legend of "Range Four Harry" and some kind of a wild "radioactive horse." Two of the witnesses confirmed the existence of "Range Four Harry" which Charles explained was the name given to a Tall White Guard who spent a lot of time at range four. The radioactive horse was, in fact, how a group of Tall White beings appeared at night, as they left the ranges gathered closely together in a group wearing their luminous, protective suits.

Another of the three witnesses added that he had relieved Charles from his duties when he finally left Indian Springs, and was told at the commencement of his duties to be observant of the UFOs, and on occasions would call the aerodrome officer at Nellis AFB when suspicious occurrences would transpire, but that the "powers that be" would never confirm any aircraft in the area.

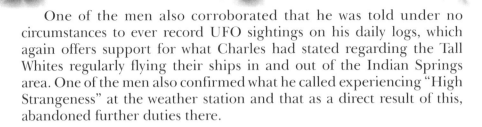

One of the men also corroborated that he was told under no circumstances to ever record UFO sightings on his daily logs, which again offers support for what Charles had stated regarding the Tall Whites regularly flying their ships in and out of the Indian Springs area. One of the men also confirmed what he called experiencing "High Strangeness" at the weather station and that as a direct result of this, abandoned further duties there.

In the *Millennial Hospitality* series, Charles mentions a substantial amount of funding concerning the building of a very large accommodation facility at Indian Springs, described as a "large hangar base" that was built to accommodate the Tall White beings and their ships in the 1950s. It's interesting to note that an article from the *Las Vegas Review Journal* dated January, 1951, describes funding for the amount of 300 million dollars that was spent in 1951 to fund a large accommodation facility, and that it was not connected with the atomic program, but tied into defense plans. Perhaps this may be the same funding Charles was referring to in his book.

Over the years, Charles has repeatedly told the same story. He defends his amazing claim that Tall White extraterrestrials inhabit a certain location of Indian Springs, and has testified to actual events and various military personnel who he discusses in his trilogy. The testimonies of the three witnesses also offer confirmation to what Charles has affirmed, and is certainly food for thought in this whole alien encounter phenomenon.

Conclusion
and Final Thoughts

Ever since my first UFO sighting in 1987, which then lead to over a dozen or more subsequent sightings over the past twenty-four years, this phenomena has not been so strange as other such bizarre and challenging parts of it that I have personally experienced throughout my life. I, like so many other individuals around the world, have encountered as a totally *different* angle to the UFO phenomena itself. Not just the witnessing of a phenomenal and extraordinary craft that is literally out-of-this-world – a solid nuts-and-bolt structure hovering in the day or night sky – but a different angle to the phenomena. This angle is the one that presents itself as an uninvited personal interaction with the occupants of the crafts themselves, physical nonhuman beings that can only be concluded to be that of either alien origin, time travelers, or possibly both.

Having personally experienced a few strange encounters myself, I feel there is no other category that these experiences can comfortably, or logically fit in to. These personal experiences of my own tied together with the experiences of the handful of credible and sane people in this book, as well as millions of other people like them around the world, has therefore left me with the realization of knowing that the reality of these alien encounters, although bizarre in nature and admittedly crazy sounding, are most definitely very *real* experiences that are taking place right here on our own spaceship, our beloved mother Earth.

Many of the highly respected clinical psychiatrists and regression therapists around the world, a handful of which are mentioned in the introduction of this book, have made many efforts to shed as much light on the alien encounter phenomena and their reproductive agenda as possible, after spending an exponential amount of valuable time with the experiencers or abductees themselves. Countless hours, days, weeks, months, sometimes even years trying to unravel and make sense of their clients' personal encounters either consciously, or through hypnotic regression.

Some encounters with the alien phenomena have been extremely invasive and have created such real emotion, anxiety, depression, and fear. It has been consistently shown that many people have reported the very same thing happening to them, time and time again, in the very same way, and more often than not with the very same grey, nonhuman-type entities. Further, according to research, evidence has been shown that these beings need humanity's help through interaction with them and their secret agenda (that is not so secret anymore). Over time, it has come to light that this agenda is for the specific purpose of their seemingly important alien-human hybrid program. It is now known that their agenda is self-centered and based around *their* goals and what *they* want to achieve from it. To date, we are still very much in the dark as to the what the extent of their agenda is or to what their full intentions are.

Where do we possibly begin to accept the unacceptable in this challenging phenomena?

What is found with experiencers and abductees in the majority is that accepting the reality of this phenomena is not only an incredibly difficult task for the individual themselves, but all too often the relationship with their spouse, partner, or family also becomes affected and altered greatly. This leaves the person who has experienced such a traumatic encounter in an extremely isolated position. They feel that they cannot easily talk about the encounter with the people they trust to understand or be accepting of their experience.

Seeking professional counseling, or joining a UFO /abduction support group is usually one of the few steps taken. Sometimes a spouse or partner will join as well (if willing), so that they can learn more about what the other is experiencing in all of this. But in some circumstances, counseling or a support group has unfortunately failed to provide the successful results needed in helping to bridge the gap of understanding and the acceptance of such a phenomena. Therefore, the marriage or relationship becomes tainted, broken and eventually may end, as accepting the unacceptable becomes too much of a challenge for the other person to handle, or to live with.

Why are certain people chosen?

Over recent years, some researchers have speculated that perhaps specific blood types played an important part in the whole alien encounter phenomena, and ultimately considered it to be a key component in contributing to the *so-called* alien-human-hybrid program. It was thought that people with a more rare blood type, such as Rhesus Negative, were the ones chosen and being targeted for the alien project. But, in fact, individuals from all over the world who have had these encounters have proven not only to be the Rhesus Negative blood type, but have had varying blood types. Because of this, research has shown that there is not one particular blood type that these beings are looking for, but that they are seeking certain "definitive characteristics" within the individual themselves that pertain to their DNA structure – their personal make-up that, for whatever reason, allows them to be the "cream of the crop" for what these beings are requiring. It's now understood that these nonhuman entities, whoever they may be, are concerned and highly interested with the importance of family lineage, and the family gene pool.

Some of the Greys have apparently become a sentient race with their advanced sciences, who seek to use their scientific technologies for their own benefit by using genetic characteristics from the human race to improve and enhance their own species. It has been speculated numerous times that their home world is indeed located within the Zeta Reticuli region, which is a binary star system in the southern constellation of Reticulum. From the southern hemisphere, the pairing stars can be seen with the naked eye as double stars in our extremely dark, night skies, and are located at a distance of approximately 39 light-years from earth – in fact, we could say just down the street!

Is there an end in sight to their project?

Best selling author David Jacob's Ph.D., of the books *Secret life* and *The Threat,* believes there to be a definite beginning, middle, and end to the alien agenda. He is of the opinion, after hypnotically regressing hundreds upon hundreds of people and through what he has uncovered during those regressions, that results suggest that the end to the alien beings' project concludes with them infiltrating our society here on Earth with the alien-human hybrids from the program. Because of this, he is not hopeful for the future of our planet, for he believes that there would be no other possible reason for aliens to create such a hybrid race if, in fact, they were not about to seed them here to co-exist with human kind.

Of the many alien encounter cases that have been reported from around the world, a considerable number of them have concluded also that they believe this to be the ultimate intention of the alien beings, and feel that something of great importance will happen soon on our planet. On the occasion, these nonhuman entities have openly shared information with the experiencer that their project will eventually come to completion, but do not specifically give a timeline, and add that they have no desire or will to take over our planet, but to simply be a part of it.

It's claimed that human-alien hybrids are already here among us, walking the earth and preparing others of their kind for their arrival and eventual residence here. We should ask ourselves two very important questions:

- Is the phenomenon then solely to do with the preservation of life here on Earth?

- Will the alien breeding program be of any benefit to human civilization?

There are numerous questions to be raised regarding this very real and challenging phenomenon, questions that most certainly outweigh the speculative answers.

Note from the Author

The author is interested in interviewing any witnesses of UFO phenomena and people who have experienced possible alien encounters, most especially children who have encountered these kinds of incidents.

Please contact her at the website:

www.letstalkparanormal.com

or her email address

Lets_talkparanormal@yahoo.com

Resources

"Abduction of Air Force Sergeant Charles L. Moody, 1975." www.ufocasebook.com.

"Abduction of Jason Andrews – 1987." www.ufocasebook.com.

"Casebook: The Abduction of Betty Andreasson Luca." BJ's Interview with Abductee Betty Andreasson Luca -UFO. www.ufocasebook.com/andreassonluca.html.

"Charles Hall & the Tall Whites." http://www.exopolitics.org/Exo-Comment-36.htm.

"Jim Weiner – The Allagash Abductions." www.ufoevidence.org/cases/case466.htm.

"The Christa Tilton Story, 1987." www.ufocasebook.com. www.thewatcherfiles.com/dulce/chapter25. htm.

"The Manhattan Abduction, UFO Casebook." http://www.ufocasebook.com/Manhattan.html.

"The Walton Experience – The Aliens." Travis Walton, http://www.travis-walton.com/aliens.html

Abduction: Human Encounters with Aliens – John E. Mack. Simon & Schuster.

Antonio Villas Boas – Abduction Episode Ground Zero. Terry Melanson – 2001.

Blue Mountains Triangle, Chapter Thirteen – "Abductions by the Energy Beings. Rex and Heather Gilroy"

Captured – The Betty and Barney Hill UFO Experience. Stanton T. Friedman, Msc., and Kathleen Marden, New Page Books.

Communion. Whitely Strieber, Avon Books, 1995.

Dechmont Woods - Abduction of Robert Taylor 1979, BJ Booth.

Roper Poll.

The Catchers of Heaven. Dr. Michael Wolf Ph.D, M.D., D.S.C.,M.S., B.S., Dorrance Publishing Co., Inc.

The Keepers; An Alien Message for the Human Race. Jim Sparks, Wild Flower Press.

The Threat. David Jacobs, Ph.D, Simon & Schuster.

Witnessed; The True Story of the Brooklyn Bridge UFO Abductions. Budd Hopkins, Bloomsbury Publishing, 1997.

Bibliography

Booth, B.J. *Dechmont Woods - Abduction of Robert Taylor 1979*. Unknown publisher/date.

Friedman, Msc., Stanton T. and Kathleen Marden. *Captured – The Betty and Barney Hill UFO Experience*. New Page Books: Franklin Lakes, NJ, 2007.

Gilroy, Rex and Heather. *Blue Mountains Triangle, Chapter Thirteen – Abductions by the Energy Beings*. URU Publications (location unknown), 2007.

Hopkins, Budd. *Witnessed: The True Story of the Brooklyn Bridge UFO Abductions*. Bloomsbury Publishing (unknown location), 1997.

Jacobs, David. *The Threat*. Simon & Schuster: New York, NY, 1998.

Mack, John E. *Abduction: Human Encounters with Aliens*. Simon & Schuster: London, UK, 1994.

Melanson, Terry. *Antonio Villas Boas – Abduction Episode Ground Zero*. Unknown publisher/location, 2001.

Roper Poll.

Sparks, Jim. *The Keepers; An Alien Message for the Human Race*. Wild Flower Press: Columbus, NC, 2006.

Strieber, Whitely. *Communion*. Wilson & Neff: New York, NY, 1987

Walton, Travis. "The Walton Experience – The Aliens." http://www.travis-walton.com/aliens.html.

Wolf, Michael, Ph.D, M.D., D.S.C., M.S., B.S. *The Catchers of Heaven* Dorrance Publishing Co., Inc.: Pittsburgh, PA, 1993 .

www.exopolitics.org/Exo-Comment-36.htm. "Charles Hall & the Tall Whites."

www.ufocasebook.com. "Abduction of Air Force Sergeant Charles L. Moody, 1975."

www.ufocasebook.com. "Abduction of Jason Andrews – 1987."

www.ufocasebook.com. www.thewatcherfiles.com/dulce/chapter25.htm."The Christa Tilton Story, 1987."

www.ufocasebook.com/andreassonluca.html. BJ's Interview with Abductee Betty Andreasson Luca. "UFO Casebook; The Abduction of Betty Andreasson Luca."

www.ufocasebook.com/Manhattan.html. "The Manhattan Abduction, UFO Casebook."

www.ufoevidence.org/cases/case466.htm. "Jim Weiner – The Allagash Abductions."

Recommended Reading

Abduction – Human Encounters with Aliens – John E. Mack

Captured! The Betty and Barney Hill UFO Experience – The True Story of the World's First Documented
    Alien Abduction - Stanton T. Friedman, Msc., and Kathleen Marden

Connecting the Dots....Making sense of the UFO Phenomenon – Paola Leopizzi Harris

Contactees – A History of Alien-Human Interaction – Nick Redfern

Extraterrestrial Visitations – True Accounts of Contact – Preston Dennett

Lost was the Key – A True Story of Alien Abduction – Leah A. Haley

Penetration – The Question of Extraterrestrial and Human Telepathy – Ingo Swann

Raechel's Eyes – The Strange But True Case of a Human-Alien Hybrid – Helen Littrell and Jean Bilodeaux

Secret Life – Firsthand Accounts of UFO Abductions – David M. Jacobs, Ph.D.

The Aliens and the Scalpel – Scientific Proof of Extraterrestrial Implants in Humans – Dr. Roger K. Leir,
    D.P.M.

The Keepers – An Alien Message for the Human Race – Jim Sparks

The Threat – David M. Jacobs, Ph.D.

UFO Crash in Brazil – A Genuine UFO Crash with Surviving ETs – Dr. Roger K. Leir, D.P.M.

UFOs...Alien Thought Machines – How the Minds of Aliens, By Thought Alone, Create and Control Their
    Space Ships – Linc W. Alexander

Recommended Websites

http://barbaralambmft.com
http://paolaharris.com
www.exopolitics.org
www.alienscalpel.com
www.intrudersfoundation.org
www.ysmith.com/index-3.html
www.ufoabduction.com